Smith Wigglesworth

—❦❦—

ON PRAYER,

POWER, AND MIRACLES

Compiled by Roberts Liardon

Smith
Wigglesworth

DESTINY IMAGE PUBLISHERS, INC
P.O. Box 310, Shippensburg, PA 17257-0310

"Speaking to the Purposes of God for This Generation and for the Generations to Come"

This book and all other Destiny Image, Revival Press, MercyPlace, Fresh Bread, Destiny Image Fiction, and Treasure House books are available at Christian bookstores and distributors worldwide.

For a U.S. bookstore nearest you, call 1-800-722-6774.

For more information on foreign distributors, call 717-532-3040.

Or reach us on the Internet: www.destinyimage.com

Library of Congress Cataloging-in-Publication Data

Wigglesworth, Smith, 1859-1947.
     Smith Wigglesworth on prayer, power, and miracles / Smith Wigglesworth; compiled by
        Roberts Liardon. -- 1st ed. p. cm.
    Includes bibliographical references.
      ISBN-10: 0-7684-2315-5
      ISBN-13: 978-0-7684-2315-0 (pbk. : alk. paper)
      1. Spiritual life--Pentecostal churches.   I. Liardon, Roberts. II. Title.
    BV4501.3.W5424 2005
    252'.0994--dc22

                            2005031561

For Worldwide Distribution, Printed in the U.S.A.

14 15 16 17 18 19 / 22 21 20 19 18

CONTENTS

SECTION TWO: THE WORKING OF MIRACLES

SECTION THREE: ULTIMATE POWER

FOREWORD

I am privileged to be the granddaughter of the "apostle of faith," my grandfather, the late Smith Wigglesworth. I remember him as a stately old gentleman immaculately dressed. His shoes were specially made—size six—and were always highly polished.

In the home, Grandfather was gentle and would weep as the younger grandchildren came in to greet him after one of his preaching tours in Britain or abroad. He would sit in his easy chair with a rug over his knees and the New Testament in his hand. He brought each of us a Newbury Bible and wrote on the front page: "Trusting that this will be the choicest of all books to you."

On Wednesday evenings my father, who was Grandfather's eldest son, and Father's two younger brothers, Ernest and Harold, would meet to sit and listen to Grandfather expound the Scriptures. He would recount some of his experiences concerning his healing ministry abroad. I was privileged to be present at some of these sittings. The presence of the Lord was so intense that I would prefer to leave the house quietly and walk through the Park, taking the quiet road home, in order not to meet people and by conversation break the holy presence of God.

At the age of 17 Grandfather asked me to stand by his chair and said, "If you surrender your life to God, He will send you all over the world." I am surprised in looking back over my life now to find how many countries I have actually visited— including New Zealand. In that beautiful country I realized my grandfather's greatness in God, through the testimonies being given. Many healings had taken place, and after 40 years the privileged people were still well. A number of people wanted to give me a hug because they were so thrilled to meet the offspring of Smith Wigglesworth—the man of God.

Grandfather died as he lived, without complaint, leaving us all a legacy of tried faith. It is my heart's desire that all who read this excellent book will be inspired to have the same fervent faith in God.

Alice Berry
Neé Wigglesworth
Granddaughter of Smith Wigglesworth

INTRODUCTION

Dr. Lester Sumrall once told me a personal story about Smith Wigglesworth that illustrates his bold and unashamed personality. He told me how Wigglesworth would frequently travel with his daughter Alice. She had a hearing problem and would often sit and listen to her father's sermons with a "hearing horn." Once, a man yelled from the audience: "Wigglesworth! If you are such a healer in the power of God, then why does your daughter need a hearing horn?" Unshaken by the question, Wigglesworth looked to the man and said, "When you can tell me why Elijah was bald, I'll tell you why Alice needs a hearing horn."

Smith Wigglesworth never minced his words, and he was never shaken by religious persecution. I admire that quality in Smith Wigglesworth. In fact, I've always loved his ministry. I am continually blessed by the mixture of his boldness, his faith, and his compassion. As I've traveled throughout the world, I've found that others have never grown tired of his ministry. Smith Wigglesworth had a true Pentecostal ministry with no man-made strings attached. Walking in an astounding measure of anointing, Wigglesworth never waited for special camp meetings to show the power of God. Instead, he daily demonstrated the book of Acts, producing countless salvations and miracles in his ministry.

While on earth, we will never have the opportunity to sit in a Wigglesworth meeting. That's one reason I am publishing this book. I want you to experience how it would have been to be a part of the congregation and receive the Word and the Spirit from Wigglesworth. I have purposely left these manuscripts in their original form. Wigglesworth's ministry shook nations and became world-renowned for the incredible strength, anointing, and insight he carried.

Many of these sermons from my private collection were recorded in shorthand by Wigglesworth's stenographers, and we've translated them into this form for publication. This book is comprised of messages that were preached in many countries around the world, including the United States, Europe, South Africa, and Australia.

In this book you will experience Smith Wigglesworth's actual ministry. You will notice that many times throughout his sermons he would inspirationally sing out melodies that came from the strength of his spirit. Other times, he would begin to speak in tongues and then interpret what the Spirit of God spoke through him. He had a wonderful habit of submitting to the Holy Spirit and yielding to the gifts of the Spirit. Though manifestations such as these are repeatedly illustrated in the New Testament, they are specifically mentioned in 1 Corinthians 12.

In my book, *God's Generals: Why They Succeeded and Why Some Failed,* I tell Wigglesworth's story in a condensed, yet very dramatic manner. In that book, his particular chapter thoroughly explains his character make-up and the challenges he faced in that generation.

Not long ago, I was in South Africa where I met with Wigglesworth's granddaughter and great-granddaughter. They are both in the ministry with their husbands, and I ministered at their church. I told them about the unpublished manuscripts I had in my possession and offered his family my complete collection for their own rights and publication usage. Recognizing my genuine love for their grandfather, and seeing the anointing God had given me to minister about these Generals, they told me to publish the sermons myself.

With their blessing and support, I dedicate these sermons, which have never been published in one book volume, to the Wigglesworth family—and to future generations of bold, aggressive reformers whose true citizenship is in heaven. May you turn the world upside down with the Kingdom of God.

Roberts Liardon

THE HEAVENLY
ORDER OF FAITH

*And so there is a higher order than the
natural man, and God wants to bring us into
this higher order, where we will believe Him.*

Later years of his life.

ROCKED IN GOD!
February 4, 1917

Hebrews 11. Faith is the evidence, the assurance that the word that God hath said is true. It is the gift of God. Unclouded faith has entered in to prove all things and believe all things. "...all men have not faith" (2 Thess. 3:2). Those of faith in God are determined that no man shall take their crown. They see the promise. See the thing there and claim it from God. It is always more than one can carry! It not only helps you, but all who believe the report. A living Word, quickened by a living faith, brings forth the evidence, which though not seen is there. Men of grace have found glory begun below.

God rocked in a man makes a man rocked in God and so submitted to God that there is no carefulness. Moses with his face-to-face communion could say, "If these men die the common death of all men...then the Lord hath not sent me" (Num. 16:29)—justice against all mourners, grumblers and unbelievers. God can so fill a man with His Spirit that he can laugh and believe in the face of a thousand difficulties. Joshua dealt with the wedge of gold and the Babylonish garment, but sin had to be removed and the saints must ever say Amen! to the judgments of God which work out His purpose. He spake and it was done, for faith is a substitutionary work of grace and an imputed righteousness. "They that trust in the Lord shall be as mount Zion, which cannot be removed, but abideth for ever" (Ps. 125:1), because they have kept His Word. Keep His Word at all costs. Faith! The substance of faith wrought out by the will of God within you, a living faith given by God. We are so saved that all things are possible. Nothing of this world existed, it was brought forth by the Word of God. Faith is creative. The walls of Jericho will fall. Abel offered his offering on the lines that God approved. If we have any faith it is through the blood of Jesus. God has respect to the blood. Will not God avenge His own elect (Luke 18:7)? Yea, I tell you, He will avenge them speedily (v. 8). Who are they? Blood-bought ones—greater than John—by faith Enoch pleased God—Peter on the mount said, "...let us make three tabernacles...there was a cloud that overshadowed them...they saw no man any more, save Jesus only..." (Mark 9:5,7,8).

Jesus is all we need. Faith is loyalty to Jesus, belief on the basis of the blood. Because of this testimony of faith God moved with Jesus.

Noah was a preacher of righteousness 120 years; he never wavered or lost the reality of God. There was no sea near, but God had said that He would send a flood. It was sufficient. The fear of God has a principle and in it brings peace. Real faith has perfect peace and joy and a shout at any time. It always sees the victory. Real faith built the ark, but real faith did not shut the door. God did that. He does what you cannot do. When they were all in, God shut the door. When God shuts no man can open. When you are all shut in, it is sure to come to pass. As the large ship on the ocean rocks in the storm, the natural man says fearfully, "Do you think we shall ever land?" but to the man of God—peace. He holdeth the sea in the hollow of His hand.

Peace, perfect peace, in this dark world of sin, in the world tribulation, but in Me, peace. The men of grace have found glory begun below. Through all the unrest of the times? Yes! "Thou wilt keep him in perfect peace, whose mind is stayed on thee..." (Isa. 26:3). "...perfect love casteth out fear... (1 John 4:18). Perfect love, perfect peace.

God said to Abraham: "Go" and he went. He was a stranger in the land, but God brought him into possession because he believed. All this is for us, for them it was natural lives, for us spiritual progress, and we are both to be perfected together. The Word of the Lord endureth forever. Did they get in? Yes! Have you? When they believed God worked out a plan. But now they desire a better country, wherefore God is not ashamed to be called their God, He hath prepared for them a city. A baptism of the Holy Ghost according to the Word.

The just shall hold constant communion with God and be so wrought upon by the Spirit and by the Spirit shall works of righteousness be manifested from strength to strength, judging all things and holding fast that which is good. "...Eye hath not seen, nor ear heard, neither have entered into the heart of man, the things which God hath prepared for them that love him. But God hath revealed them unto us by his Spirit: for the Spirit searcheth all things, yea, the deep things of God" (1 Cor. 2:9,10). A substance of faith beyond all that has gone before—they desire a better country—that is, a heavenly. They saw— were persuaded—embraced—confessed, i.e., they lived in the power of them. Truly, beloved, God hath prepared for us wonderful things.

Address given at Rowland Street Mission

The Wigglesworth family: Top row (left to right) Alice, Seth, and Harold
Bottom row (left to right) Ernest, Smith, Polly, and George

DETHRONING UNBELIEF
October –December 1919

*Then said they unto him, What shall we do, that we might work the
works of God? Jesus answered and said unto them, This is the work
of God, that ye believe on him whom he hath sent.*

John 6:28,29

"This is the work of God, that ye believe." Nothing in the world
glorifies God so much as simple rest of faith in what God's Word says.
Jesus said, "...My Father worketh hitherto, and I work" (John 5:17). He
saw the way the Father did the works; it was on the ground- work of
knowledge, faith based upon knowledge. When I know Him, there are
any amount of promises I can lay hold of, then there is no struggle, "For
[he] that asketh receiveth; and he that seeketh findeth; and to him that
knocketh it shall be opened" (Matt. 7:8).

Jesus lived to manifest God's glory in the earth, to show forth what
God was like, that many sons might be brought to glory (Heb. 2:10).

John the Baptist came as a forerunner, testifying beforehand to the
coming revelation of the Son. The Son came, and in the power of the
Holy Ghost revealed faith. The Living God has chosen us in the midst of
His people. The power is not of us, but of God. Yes, beloved, it is the
power of another within us.

THE SON OF GOD

Just in the measure we are clothed and covered and hidden in Him, is His inner working manifested. Jesus said, "...My Father worketh hitherto, and I work" (John 5:17). Oh, the joy of the knowledge of it!—to know Him. We know if we look back how God has taken us on. We love to shout "Hallelujah," pressed out beyond measure by the Spirit, as He brings us face to face with reality, His blessed Holy Spirit dwelling in us and manifesting the works. I must know the sovereignty of His grace and the manifestation of His power. Where am I? I am in Him; He is in God. The Holy Ghost, the great Revealer of the Son. Three persons dwelling in man. The Holy Spirit is in us for revelation to manifest the Christ of God. Therefore be it known unto you, He that dwelleth in God doeth the works (John 14:10). The law of the Spirit of life having made us free from the law of sin and death (Rom. 8:2).

The Spirit working in righteousness, bringing us to the place where

ALL UNBELIEF IS DETHRONED

and Christ is made the head of the Corner. "...this is the Lord's doing, and it is marvellous in our eyes" (Matt. 21:42). It is a glorious fact, we are in God's presence, possessed by Him; we are not our own, we are clothed with Another. What for? For the deliverance of the people. Many can testify to the day and hour when they were delivered from sickness by a supernatural power. Some would have passed away with influenza if God had not intervened, but God stepped in with a new revelation, showing us we are born from above, born by a new power, God dwelling in us superseding the old. "If ye shall ask any thing in my name, I will do it" (John 14:14). Ask and receive, and your joy shall be full, if ye dare to believe (John 16:24). "...What shall we do, that we might work the works of God? This is the work of God, that ye believe on him whom he hath sent" (John 6:28,29). God is more anxious to answer than we are to ask. I am speaking of faith based upon knowledge.

A TESTIMONY

I was healed of appendicitis, and that because of the knowledge of it; faith based upon the knowledge of the experience of it. Where I have ministered to others, God has met and answered according to His will. It is in our trust and our knowledge of the power of God—the knowledge that God will not fail us if we will only believe. "...speak the word only, and my servant shall be healed" (Matt. 8:8). Jesus said unto the centurion, "Go thy way; as thou hast believed, so be it done unto thee. And his servant was healed in the selfsame hour" (Matt. 8:13).

AN INSTANCE

In one place where I was staying a young man came in telling us his sweetheart was dying; there was no hope. I said, "Only believe." What was it? Faith based upon knowledge. I knew that what God had done for me He could do for her. We went to the house. Her sufferings were terrible to witness. I said, "In the name of Jesus come out of her." She cried, "Mother, Mother, I am well." Then I said that the only way to make us believe it was to get up and dress. Presently she came down dressed. The doctor came in and examined her carefully. He said, "This is of God; this is the finger of God." It was faith based upon knowledge.

If I received a check for £1000, and knew only imperfectly the character of the man that sent it, I should be careful of the man that sent it, I should be careful not to reckon on it until it was honored. Jesus did great works because of His knowledge of His Father. Faith begets knowledge, fellowship, communion. If you see imperfect faith, full of doubt, a wavering condition, it always comes of

IMPERFECT KNOWLEDGE.

Jesus said,

Father...I knew that thou hearest me always: but because of the people which stand by I said it, that they may believe that thou hast sent me...he cried with a loud voice, Lazarus, come forth.

John 11:41-43

And God wrought special miracles by the hands of Paul: so that from his body were brought unto the sick handkerchiefs or aprons, and the diseases departed from them, and the evil spirits went out of them.

Acts 19:11,12

For our conversation is in heaven from whence also we look for the Savior.

Who shall fashion anew the body of our humiliation that it may be conformed to the body of His glory, according to the working whereby He is able to subdue all things unto Himself? How God has cared for me these 12 years, and blessed me, giving me such a sense of His presence! When we depend upon God how bountiful He is, giving us enough and to spare for others. Lately God has enabled me to take victory on new lines, a living-in-Holy Ghost attitude in a new way. As we meet, immediately the glory falls. The Holy Ghost has the latest news from the Godhead, and has designed for us the right place at the right time. Events happen in a remarkable way. You drop in where the need is.

There have been several mental cases lately. How difficult they are naturally, but how easy for God to deal with. One lady came, saying, "Just over the way there is a young man terribly afflicted,

DEMENTED

with no rest day or night." I went with a very imperfect knowledge as to what I had to do, but in the weak places God helps our infirmities. I rebuked the demon in the name of Jesus, then I said, "I'll come again tomorrow." Next day when I went he was with his father in the field and quite well.

Another case. Fifty miles away there was a fine young man, 25 years of age. He had lost his reason, could have no communication with his mother, and he was always wandering up and down. I knew God was waiting to bless. I cast out the demon-power, and heard long after he had become quite well. Thus the blessed Holy Spirit takes us on from one place to another. So many things happen, I live in heaven on earth. Just the other day, at Coventry, God relieved the people. Thus He takes us on and on and on.

Do not wait for inspiration if you are in need; the Holy Ghost is here, and you can have perfect deliverance as you sit in your seats.

I was taken to three persons, one in care of an attendant. As I entered the room there was a terrible din, quarreling, such a noise it seemed as if all the powers of hell were stirred. I had to wait God's time. The Holy Ghost rose in me at the right time, and the three were delivered, and at night were singing praises to God. There had to be activity and testimony. Let it be known unto you this Man Christ is the same today. Which man? God's Man Who has to have the glory, power, and dominion. "For he must reign, till he hath put all enemies under his feet" (1 Cor. 15:25). When He reigns in you, you know how to obey, how to work in conjunction with His will, His power, His light, His life, having faith based upon knowledge, we know He has come. "...ye shall receive power, after that the Holy Ghost is come upon you..." (Acts 1:8). We are in the experience of it.

Sometimes a live word comes unto me, in the presence of a need, a revelation of the Spirit to my mind, "Thou shalt be loosed." Loosed now? It looks like presumption, but God is with the man who dares to stand upon His Word. I remember, for instance, a person who had not been able to smell anything for four years. I said, "You will smell now if you believe." This stirred another who had not smelled for 20 years. I said, "You will smell tonight." She went about smelling everything, and was quite excited. Next day she gave her testimony. Another came and asked, "Was it possible for God to heal her ears?" The drums were removed. I said, "Only believe." She went down into the audience in great distress; others were healed, but she could not hear. The next night she came again. She said, "I am going to believe tonight." The glory fell. The first time she came feeling; the second time she came believing.

At one place there was a man anointed for [a] rupture. He came the next night, rose in the meeting saying, "This man is an impostor; he is deceiving the people. He told me last night I was healed; I am worse than ever today." I spoke to the evil power that held the man and rebuked it, telling the man he was indeed healed. He was a mason. Next day he testified to lifting heavy weights, and that God had met him. "...with his stripes we are healed" (Isa. 53:5). He hath made to light on Him the iniquity of us all. It was the Word of God, not me he was against.

"...What shall we do, that we might work the works of God? Jesus answered and said unto them, This is the work of God, that ye believe on him whom he hath sent" (John 6:28,29). Anything else? Yes. He took our infirmities and healed all our diseases. I myself am a marvel of healing. If I fail to glorify God, the stones would cry out.

Salvation is for all,
Healing is for all.
Baptism of the Holy Ghost is for all.

21

Reckon yourselves dead indeed unto sin, but alive unto God.
By His grace get the victory every time. It is possible to live holy.
He breaks the power of canceled sin,
He sets the prisoner free;
His blood can make the foulest clean,
His blood avails for me.

*...What shall we do, that we might work the works of God? Jesus
answered and said unto them, This is the work of God, that ye
believe on him whom he hath sent.*

John 6:28,29

Published in *Confidence*

FINDING THE HIGHER ORDER OF FAITH
1922

The Lord give us patience to take in this Word. It is a very marvelous Word, and God wants us to fully comprehend the fullness of what it means to us all. The great plan of God's salvation is redemption in its fullness.

There are things in this chapter that will bring a revelation of what God means for the man who believes. While I know prayer is wonderful, and not only changes things but changes you, while I know the man of prayer can go right in and take the blessing from God, yet I tell you that if we grasp this truth that we have before us, we shall find that faith is the greatest inheritance of all.

May God give us faith that will bring this glorious inheritance into our hearts; for, beloved, it is true that the just shall live by faith; and do not forget that it takes a just man to live by faith, and may the Lord reveal to us the fullness of this truth that God gave to Abraham.

THAT BLESSED PLACE

Twenty-five years Abraham had the promise that God would give him a son. Twenty-five years he stood face to face with God on the promise, expecting every year to have a son. There was Sarah becoming weaker and his own stamina and body becoming more frail, and natural conditions so changing both Sarah and him that, so far as they could see, there was no such thing as seeing their bodies bring forth fruit. And, if they had looked at their bodies as some people do theirs, they would probably have remained like they were forever. But Abraham dared not look either at Sarah or himself in that respect. He had to look at God. You cannot find anywhere that God ever failed. And He wants to bring us into that blessed place of faith, changing us into a real substance of faith, till we are so like-minded that whatever we ask we believe we receive, and our joy becomes full because we believe. I want you to see how God covered Abraham because he believed.

Hear what God said to Abraham, and then see how Abraham acts. He was amongst his own people and his own kindred, and God said to him, "Come out, Abraham, come out!" And Abraham obeyed, and came out, not knowing whither he was going. You say, "He was the biggest ass that ever God had under His hands." You will never go through with God on any lines except by believing Him. It is, "Thus saith the Lord" every time; and you will see the plan of God come right through when you dare believe. He came right out of his own country, and God was with him. Because he believed God, God overshadowed him. I am as confident as possible that if we could get to the place of believing God, we need not have a dog in the yard or a lock on the door. All this is unbelief. God is able to manage the whole business. It doesn't matter how many thieves are about; they cannot break through nor steal where God is.

I want, by the help of God, to lead you into the truth, for there is nothing but the truth can set you free, but truth can always do it. It is impossible, if God covers you with His righteousness, for anything to happen to you, contrary to the mind of God.

When God sets His seal upon you, the devil dare not break it. He dare not break in where you are. You know what a "seal" is, don't you? Now, then, when God puts His seal upon you, the devil has no power there. He dare not break that seal and go through; and God puts His seal upon the man that believes Him. There are two kinds of righteousness. There is a righteousness that is according to the law, the keeping of the law; but there is a better righteousness than that. You ask, "What could be better than keeping the law"? The righteousness that sees God and obeys Him in everything! The righteousness that believes that every prayer uttered is going to bring the answer from God. There is a righteousness that is made known only to the heart that knows God. There is a side to the inner man that God can reveal only to the man who believes Him.

We have any amount of scriptural illustrations to show us how God worked with those people who believed Him. I have any amount of definite instances in my life where God came, where God was, where God worked, where God planned. And here is one of the greatest plans of all, where God works in this man (Abraham) exactly opposite to human nature. There were many good points about Sarah, but she had not reached the place. She laughed, and then denied having done so, and when they waited a time and she saw that their bodies were growing frailer, she said: "Now it will be just as good for you to take Hagar for a wife and bring forth a son through her." But that was not the seed of Abraham that God spoke about, and that caused a great deal of trouble in the house of Abraham; and there are times when you dare not take your wife's advice. The man who walks with God can only afford to take God's leadings, and when He leads you it is direct and clear, and the evidence is so real that every day you know that God is with you unfolding His plan to you. It is lovely to be in the will of God.

TONGUES AND INTERPRETATION: "Glory to God! He is the Lord of Hosts Who cometh forth into the heart of the human life of man, and speaks according to His divine plan, and as you live in the Spirit, you live in the process of God's mind, and act according to His divine will."

A HIGHER ORDER

And so there is a higher order than the natural man, and God wants to bring us into this higher order, where we will believe Him. In the first place, God promised Abraham a son. Could a child be born into the world, except on the line of the natural law? It was when all natural law was finished, and when there was no substance in these two persons, that the law of the Spirit brought forth a son. It was the law of faith in God Who had promised.

And then we are brought to the time when our blessed Lord was conceived. I hear Mary saying to the angel, "Lord, be it unto me according to thy word" (Luke 1:38), so that the man Christ Jesus was brought forth on the same lines. Tonight I see before me faces I know, and I can see that these men are born, not of blood, neither by the will of the flesh, but of God. We have the same law in our midst tonight. Born of God! And sometimes I see that this power within us is greater when we are weak than when we are strong; and this power was greater in Abraham day by day than when he was strong.

Looking at him, Sarah would shake her head and say: "I never saw anybody so thin and weak and helpless in my life. No, Abraham, I have been looking at you, and you seem to be going right down." But Abraham refused to look at his own body or that of Sarah; he believed the promise that it should be. Some of you people have come for healing. You know as well as possible that, according to the natural life, there is no virtue in your body to give you that health. You know also that the ailment from which you suffer has so drained your life and energy that there is no help at all in you; but God says that you shall be healed if you believe. It makes no difference how your body is. It was exactly the helplessness of Sarah and Abraham that brought the glorious fact that a son was born, and I want you to see what sort of a son he was.

He was the son of Abraham. The seed of the whole, believing church—his seed as innumerable as the sands upon the seashore. God wants you to know tonight that there is no limitation with Him, and to bring us to a place where there will be no limitation in us. This state would be brought about by the working of the Omnipotent in the human body; working in us continually—greater than any science or any power in the world—and bringing us into the place to comprehend God and man.

I want you to see tonight that Romans 4:16 has a great touch for us all. You look at it: "Therefore it is of faith, that it might be by grace; to the end the promise might be sure to all the seed; not to that only which is of the law, but to that also which is of the faith of Abraham; who is the father of us all." Think about those words, "Therefore it is of faith, that it might be by grace." Some of you would like a touch in your bodies; some would like a touch in your spirit; some would like to be baptized in the Holy Ghost; some want to be filled with all God's power. There it is for you.

> *That the blessing of Abraham might come on the Gentiles through Jesus Christ; that we might receive the promise of the Spirit through faith.*
>
> *Galatians 3:14*

Now come on the lines of faith again. I want you to see tonight that you can be healed if you will hear the Word. Now there are some people here for healing; maybe some want salvation, maybe others want sanctification and the baptism of the Spirit. This Word says it is by faith that it might be by grace. Grace is omnipotence; it is activity, benevolence, and mercy. It is truth, perfection, and God's inheritance in the soul that can believe. God gives us a negative side. What is it? It is by faith. Grace is God. You open the door by faith, and God comes in with all you want, and it cannot be otherwise, for it is "of faith, that it might be by grace." It cannot be by grace unless you say it shall be so.

This is believing, and most people want healing by feeling. It cannot be. Some even want salvation on the same lines, and they say, "Oh, if I could feel I was saved, brother!" It will never come that way. There are three things that work together. The first is faith. Faith can always bring a fact, and a fact can always bring joy, and so God brings you into this meeting to hear the Scriptures, which can make you wise unto salvation, which can open your understanding and make you so that if you will hear the truth, you will go out with what you want so that you have power to shut the door and power to open the door. Let us now take another verse more mighty still, step by step, and you will find it is very wonderful.

GOD IS

Here is Sarah—her body is dead—and Abraham—his body is dead. "As it is written, I have made thee a father of many nations... (Rom. 4:17). "Now," says Abraham, "God has made me a father of many nations, and there is no hope of a son according to the natural law—no hope whatever." But here God says, "I have made thee a father of many nations," and yet he has no son, and during the past 20 years of waiting, conditions have grown more and more hopeless, and yet the promise was made. Now how long have you been with your rheumatism and believing? How long have you been waiting for the promise and it has not come? Had you need to wait? Look here! I want to tell you that all the people who are saved are blessed with faithful Abraham. Abraham is the great substance of the whole keynote of Scripture—a man that dared for 25 years [to] believe God when everything went worse every day. Oh, it is lovely. It is perfect. I do not know anything in the Scriptures so marvelous, so far-reaching, and so full of the substance of living reality, to change us if we will believe God. He will make us so different. This blessed incarnation of living faith which changes us and makes us know that God is, and that He is a rewarder of them that diligently seek Him. God is a reality. God is true, and in Him there is no lie, neither shadow of turning. Oh, it is good! I do love to think about such truths as this.

Oh, beloved, there is not a subject in the whole Bible that makes my body aflame with passion after God and His righteousness as this. I see He never fails. He wants the man to believe, and then the man shall never fail. Oh, the loveliness of the character of God!

"The father of many nations!" You talk about your infirmities... look at this! I have never felt I have had an infirmity since I understood this chapter. Oh God, help me. I feel more like weeping than talking tonight. My cup runneth over as I see the magnitude of this living God. "(As it is written, I have made thee a father of many nations,) before him whom he believed, even God, who quickeneth the dead, and calleth those things which be not as though they were." "I won't look at my body. I won't look at my infirmities. I believe God will make the whole thing right. What matter if I have not heard for over 20 years? I believe my ears will be perfect." God is reality, and wants us to know that if we will believe it shall be perfect. "Who quickeneth that which is dead, and calleth those things which be not as though they were." No limitation of possibility. Then God tested them still further than that. Oh, it is blessed to know you are tested. It is the greatest thing in the world to be tested. You never know what you are made of till you are tested. Some people say, "Oh, I don't know why my lot is such a heavy one," and God puts them into the fire again. He knows how to do it. I can tell you, He is a blessed God. There is not such a thing as a groan when God gets hold of you. There is no such thing as want to them who trust the Lord. When we really get in the will of God, He can make our enemies to be at peace with us. It is wonderful.

Brothers, I wonder if you really believe that God can quicken that which is dead? I have seen it any amount of times. The more there was no hope, Abraham believed in hope. Sometimes satan will blear your minds and interfere with your perception that would bring right in between you and God the obscure condition; but God is able to change the whole position if you will let Him have a chance. Turn your back on every sense of unbelief, and believe God. There are some who would like to feel the presence of the touch of God; God will bring it to you. Now, I wish people could come to this place. Oh, Abraham had a good time; the more he was squeezed, the more he rejoiced; and being not weak in faith, he considered not his own body, which was now dead, when he was about 100 years old, neither yet the deadness of Sarah's womb. He staggered not through unbelief, but was strong in faith, giving God the glory (Rom. 4:19,20). God knows. He has a plan. He has a way. Dare you trust Him? He knows.

I am here—saved by the power of God because of the promise that God made to Abraham; as the countless sands upon the seashore and as the stars in multitude and glory, the seed of thy son shall be! It is for us tonight, beloved. The Scripture says to us that the delaying of the promise and the testing of Abraham was the seed of all the world to be who believed in God. And, being fully persuaded that, what He had promised He was able also to perform. Therefore, it was imputed unto him for righteousness, and not to him only, but to all the people who will believe God (Rom. 4:21-24).

THE SEED OF THE PROMISE
AND THE SEED OF THE FLESH

We have another place in the Scriptures, and I want to touch this now. Isaac was born. And you find that, right in that house where Isaac was and where Ishmael was, there was the seed of promise and the seed of flesh; and you find there is strife and trouble right there, for Ishmael was teasing Isaac. And you will find, my dear friends, as sure as anything, there is nothing that is going to hold you except the Isaac life—the seed of Abraham. You will find that the flesh-life will always have to be cast out. "And Sarah said, Cast out Hagar and her son." It was very hard to do, but it had to be done. You say, "How hard!" Yes, but how long had it to be? Till submission came! There will always be jealousy and strife in your hearts and lives till flesh is destroyed—till Isaac controls and rules in authority over the whole body; and when Isaac—power reigns over you, you will find that the whole of your life is full of peace and joy. And then comes the time when this son grew up a fine young man, perhaps twenty years of age—we are not told—but then came another test. God says to Abraham, "Take thy son Isaac, and offer him to Me upon the mount that I will shew thee." Do you think that Abraham told anybody of that? No, I am sure he didn't. He was near to his heart, and God said he had to offer him on the altar, and there he was—Isaac, the heart of his heart—and God said he was to be the seed of all living. What had he to do but to believe that, just as miraculously as Isaac came into the world, God could even raise him though he were slain. Did he tell Sarah about the thing? No, I am certain he did not, or else he would not have got away with that boy. There would have been such a trial in the home. I believe he kept it to himself. When God tells you a secret don't tell anyone else. God will, perchance, tell you to go and lay hands on some sick one. Go, do it, and don't tell anyone.

One thing I know is that satan does not know my thoughts; he only knows what I let out of my mouth. Sometimes he suggests thoughts in order to get to know, but I can see that God can captivate my thoughts in such a way that they may be entirely for Him. When God gets upon your hearts you will see that every thought is captive, that everything is brought into obedience, and is brought into a place where you are in dominion because Christ is enthroned in your life (2 Cor. 10:4,5). Some people God reveals deep and special things to. Keep your counsel before God.

Now, beloved, I see this: Abraham could offer Isaac. Now tell me how. I believe in this meeting that God wants me to tell you how, in order that you may know something about your trials. Some think they are tried more than other people. If you knew the value of it, you would praise God for trial more than for anything. It is the trial that is used to purify you; it is in the fiery furnace of affliction that God gets you in the place where He can use you. The person that has no trials and no difficulties is the person whom God dare not allow satan to touch, because he could not stand temptation; but Jesus will not allow any man to be tempted more than he is able to bear. The Scriptures are the strongest evidence of anything you can have. Before Abraham offered Isaac he was tried, and God knew he could do it. And before God puts you through the furnace of afflictions, He knows you will go through. Not one single temptation cometh to any man more than he is able to bear; and with the temptation God is always there to help you through. Don't you see that was exactly the position in the case of Abraham?

If you know you need the baptism of the Holy Spirit, and you know it is in the Scriptures, never rest till God gives it [to] you. If you know it is scriptural for you to be healed of every weakness, never rest until God makes it yours. If you know that the Scriptures teach holiness, purity, and divine likeness—overcoming under all conditions—never rest till you are an overcomer. If you know that men have gone in and have seen the face of God, who have had the vision revealed, have had the whole of the Scriptures made life in their lives, never rest till you come to it. You say, "Have you a Scripture to prove it?" Yes, the Scripture says, That ye may apprehend with all saints what is the depth, length, breadth and height of the love of God (Eph. 3:18,19).

TONGUES AND INTERPRETATION: "Oh, hallelujah! This blessed inheritance of the Spirit is come to profit withal; teaching you all things, and making you understand the will of God cometh not by observation; but holy men of old spoke and wrote as the Spirit gave them power and utterance, and so today the Holy Ghost must fill us with this same initiative of God."

We must live in the fire; we must hate sin; we must love righteous-ness; we must live with God, for He says we have to be blameless and harmless amidst the crooked positions of the world. Beloved, I look at you tonight, and I say God is able to confirm all I have been speaking about trials and testings, which are the greatest blessings you can have. God wants to make sons everywhere like unto Jesus. Jesus was a type of the sonship that we have to attain unto. I don't know how I feel when I am speaking about the loftiness of the character of Jesus, Who was a firstfruit to make us pure and holy. And I see Jesus going about clothed with power. I see likewise, every child of God in this place clothed with power, and I see every detail. Jesus was just the firstfruit—and I know that is the pattern of God.

God has not given us a pattern which would be impossible to copy. Beloved, He hated sin—which is the greatest luxury we can have in our lives. If I have a hatred for sin, I have something which is worth millions of pounds. Oh, the blood of Jesus Christ, God's Son, cleanseth us from all sin. Beloved, I feel somehow that that is the hope of the church for the future—being purified, made like unto Jesus, pure in heart, pure in thought. Then when you lay your hands upon the sick, satan has no power. When you command him to leave, he has to go. What a redemption! What a baptism! What an unction! It is ecstasies of delight beyond all expression for the soul to live and move in Him Who is our being.

Address given at Good News Hall
Melbourne, Australia

PREPARING YOURSELF TO RECEIVE FROM GOD

August 1, 1922

God will do great things for us if we are prepared to receive them from Him. We are dull of comprehension because we let the cares of this world blind our eyes, but if we keep open to God, He has a greater plan for us in the future than we have seen or ever have dreamed about in the past. It is God's delight to fulfill to us impossibilities because of His omnipotence, and when we reach the place where He alone has the right of way in all things, then all mists and misunderstandings will clear away.

I have been asking the Lord for His message for you this morning, and I believe He would have me turn to the second epistle of Peter, first chapter, beginning with the first verse:

> *Simon Peter, a servant and an apostle of Jesus Christ, to them that have obtained like precious faith with us through the righteousness of God and our Saviour Jesus Christ: Grace and peace be multiplied unto you through the knowledge of God, and of Jesus our Lord, According as his divine power hath given unto us all things that pertain unto life and godliness, through the knowledge of him that hath called us to glory and virtue: Whereby are given unto us exceeding great and precious promises: that by these ye might be partakers of*

the divine nature, having escaped the corruption that is in the world through lust. And beside this, giving all diligence, add to your faith virtue; and to virtue knowledge; and to knowledge temperance; and to temperance patience; and to patience godliness; And to godliness brotherly kindness; and to brotherly kindness charity. For if these things be in you, and abound, they make you that ye shall neither be barren nor unfruitful in the knowledge of our Lord Jesus Christ.

2 Peter: 1-8

Probably there is not a greater word that anyone could bring to an audience than this word, "like precious faith." "Like Precious Faith" means that God, who is from everlasting to everlasting, has always had people that He could trust; that He could illuminate, that He could enlarge until there was nothing within them that would hinder the power of God. Now this "Precious Faith" is the gift that God is willing to impart to all of us. He wants us to have this faith in order that we may "subdue kingdoms," "work righteousness," and, if it should be necessary, "stop the mouths of lions" (Heb. 11:33).

We should be able under all circumstances to triumph. Not that we have any help in ourselves, but our help comes only from God, and if our help is only in God then we are always strong and never weak. It is always those people who are full of faith who have a "good report," who never murmur, who are in the place of victory, who are not in the place of human order, but of divine order in God. He is the Author of our faith, and our faith is always based on "thus saith the Lord."

This "Like Precious Faith" is for all. There is a word in the third chapter of Ephesians which is very good for us to consider: that you "may be able to comprehend with all saints..." (Eph. 3:18). What does this "Like Precious Faith" mean to you this morning? Every one here is receiving a blessing because of the faith of Abraham. But remember this, this "Like Precious Faith" is the same that Abraham had. "Like Precious Faith" is the substance of the power of eternal life which is given to us through the Word. You may not be able to use this faith because of some hindrance in your life. I have had 1,000 road engines come over my life to break me up and bring me to the place where this faith could operate within me. There is no way into the deep things of God, only through a broken spirit. When we are thus broken, we cease forever from our own works for Another, even Christ, has taken the reign. Faith in God, and power with God, come to us through the knowledge of the Word of God. Whatever we may think about it, it is true that we are no better than our faith. Whatever your estimation is of your own ability, of your own righteousness, or of your work in any way, you are no better than your faith.

How wonderful is this faith that overcomes the world! "He that believeth that Jesus is the Son of God overcomes the world!" But how does he overcome the world? If you believe in Him you are purified as He is pure. You are strengthened because He is strong. You are made whole because He is whole. All of His fullness may come into you because of the revelation of Himself. Faith is the living principle of the Word of God. If we yield ourselves up to be led by the Holy Spirit we shall be divinely led into the deep things of God, and the truths and revelations and all His mind will be made so clear unto us that we shall live by faith in Christ.

God has no thought of anything on a small scale. In the passage which we have read this morning are these words, "Grace and peace be 'multiplied' unto you through the knowledge of God, and of Jesus our Lord" (2 Pet. 1:2). God's Word is always on the line of multiplication, and so I believe the Lord wants us on that line this morning. We see "Like Precious Faith" is to be obtained "through the righteousness of God and our Savior Jesus Christ." God's Word is without change. We are to be filled with the righteousness of God on the authority of the Word. His righteousness is from everlasting to everlasting, the same, yesterday and today and forever.

If I limit the Lord, He cannot work within me, but if I open myself to God then He will surely fill me and flow through me.

We must have this "Like Precious Faith" in order to have our prayers answered. If we ask anything according to God's will, we are told that He hears us, and if we know that He hears us, then we know we have the petitions that we desire. Oh, brothers, sisters, we must go into the presence of God and get from Him the answer to our prayers. Hear what Mark 11:24 says,

> ...*What things soever ye desire, when ye pray, believe that ye receive them, and ye shall have them.*

In verse 23 we see mountains removed, difficulties all cleared away. When? When the man believes in his heart and refuses to doubt. We must have the reality, we must know God, we must be able to go into His presence and converse with God.

This "Like Precious Faith" goes on multiplying in grace and in peace through the knowledge of God. It places our feet on the Rock, and brings us to an unlimited place in our faith. This faith makes you dare to do anything with and for God. Remember that you can only be built up on the Word of God. If you build yourself on imagination or your own thoughts you will go wrong.

The Bible is the Word of God: supernatural in origin, eternal in duration, inexpressible in valor, infinite in scope, regenerative in power, infallible in authority, universal in interest, personal in application, inspired in totality. Read it through, write it down, pray it in, work it out, and then pass it on. Truly it is the Word of God. It brings into man the personality of God; it changes the man until he becomes the epistle of God. It transforms his mind, changes his character, takes him on from grace to grace, and gives him an inheritance in the Spirit. God comes in, dwells in, walks in, talks through, and sups with him.

Your peace be multiplied! You are to rejoice greatly. Oh! the bride ought to rejoice to hear the Bridegroom's voice. How we love our Bridegroom and how He loves us! How adorable He is and how sweet is His countenance. At the presence of Jesus, all else goes.

Oh, my brother, my sister, we have the greatest tide of all our life. There is no tide like the power of the "latter rain." We must not fail to see what remarkable things God has for every one of us.

Beloved, I would like to press into your heart this morning the truth that God has no room for an ordinary man. God wants to take the ordinary man and put him through the sieve and bring him out into a place of extraordinary faith. The cry of our souls can be satisfied only with God. The great plan of God is to satisfy you, and then give you the vision of something higher.

If ever you stop at any point, pick up at the place where you failed, and begin again under the refining light and power and zeal of heaven and all things will be brought to you, for He will condescend to meet you.

Remember, beloved, it is not what you are but what God wants you to be. What shall we do? Shall we not dedicate ourselves afresh to God? Every new revelation brings a new dedication.

Let us seek Him.

Sermon preached at Glad Tidings Tabernacle and Bible Training School
San Francisco, California

Polly Wigglesworth

ENLARGING YOUR SOUL
BY THE WORD
August 2, 1922

TONGUES AND INTERPRETATION: "Fear not, neither be thou dismayed, for the God who has led, shall descend upon thee, shall surely carry thee where thou wouldst not. But to this end He has called thee out to take thee on, to move upon thee with divine unction of the Spirit that thou shouldst not be entertained by nature, but caught up with Him to hear His words, to speak His truth, to have His mind, to know His will, to commune and be still, to see Him who is invisible, to be able to pour out to others the great stream of life, to quicken everything wherever it moves. For the Spirit is not given by measure but He is given to us by faith, the measureless measure that we may know Him, and the power of His resurrection in the coming day. And now is the day set for us which is the opening for the coming day."

I believe the Lord would have me speak to you this morning the lines of faith, so I shall read a few verses to you from Hebrews 11:

Now faith is the substance of things hoped for, the evidence of things not seen. For by it the elders obtained a good report. Through faith we understand that the worlds were framed by the word of God, so that things which are seen were not made of things which do appear.

By faith Abel offered unto God a more excellent sacrifice than Cain, by which he obtained witness that he was righteous, God testifying of his gifts: and by it he being dead yet speaketh. By faith Enoch was translated that he should not see death; and was not found, because God had translated him: for before his translation he had this testimony, that he pleased God. But without faith it is impossible to please him: for he that cometh to God must believe that he is, and that he is a rewarder of them that diligently seek him.

Hebrews 11:1-6

I think that is as far as we will be able to get this morning. I have been much complexed whether I should continue the yesterday morning subject, but the Lord seems to turn that into this channel this morning. So may the Lord open unto us today His good treasures.

You know, beloved, that there are many wonderful treasures in the storehouse of God that we have not yet gotten. But praise God, we have the promise in Corinthians,

...Eye hath not seen, nor ear heard, neither have entered into the heart of man, the things which God hath prepared for them that love him.

1 Corinthians 2:9

I pray God, this morning, that there may be within us a deep hunger and thirst with the penetration that is centered entirely upon the axle of Him, for surely He is all and in all. I pray God that we may be able to understand the opening of this chapter.

Now faith is the substance of things hoped for, the evidence of things not seen. For by it the elders obtained a good report. Through faith we understand that the worlds were framed by the word of God, so that things which are seen were not made of things which do appear.

Hebrews 11:1-3

Now beloved, you will clearly see this morning, that God wants to bring us to a foundation. If we are ever going to make any progress in divine life we shall have to have a real foundation. And there is no foundation, only the foundation of faith for us.

All our movements, and all that ever will come to us, which is of any importance, will be because we have a *Rock*. And if you are on the Rock, no powers can move you. And the need of today is the Rock to have our faith firm upon.

On any line of principle of your faith you must have something established in you to bring that forth. And there is no establishment outside God's Word for you. Everything else is sand. Everything else shall sunder.

If you build upon anything else but the Word of God, on imaginations, sentimentality, or any feelings, or any special joy, it will mean nothing without you have a foundation, and the foundation will have to be in the Word of God.

I was once going on a tram from L—— to Blackpool. It is one of our fashionable resorts, and many people go there because of the high tides, and the wonderful sights they get as the ocean throws up its large, massive mountain of sea.

When we were going on the tram, I looked over and said to a builder, "The men are building those houses upon the sands." "Oh," he said, "you don't know. You are not a builder. Don't you know that we can pound that sand till it becomes like rock?" I said, "Nonsense!"

I saw the argument was not going to profit, so I dropped it. By and by we reached Blackpool where the mountainous waves come over. I was looking and taking notice of so many things. I saw a row of houses that had fallen flat, and drawing the attention of this man I said, "Oh, look at those houses. See how flat they are." He forgot our previous conversation, saying, "You know here we have very large tides, and these houses being on the sands, when the floods came, they fell."

Beloved, it won't do. We must have something better than sand, and everything is sand except the Word. There isn't anything that will remain—we are told the heaven and earth will be melted up as a scroll as fervent heat. But we are told the Word of God shall be forever, and not one jot or tittle of the Word of God shall fail. And if there is anything that is satisfying me today more than another, it is, "...thy word is settled in heaven" (Ps. 119:89).

And another Word in the 138th Psalm says, "...thou hast magnified thy word above all thy name" (v. 2). The very establishment for me is the Word of God. It is not on any other line. Let us come to the principle of it. If you turn to John's gospel you will find a wonderful word there. It is worth our notice and great consideration this morning.

I would like to see more Bibles than I see. It is important. If I left my house without my purse, I should naturally return for it because it might be of importance. My brothers, your Bible is worth ten million purses and their contents, and you had better turn back for your Testament or Bible, rather than for your purse. It is more important that you have the Word of life.

Some people say, "I have it inside." People are not satisfied sometimes. You must give them chapter and verse, and ask them to read it for themselves. It is important that the people should know and we ought to be able to give a good account always of the hope that is within us.

Now beloved, I would turn to this first chapter of John this morning for a moment, for our edification, because it will help us so much. I want to make a real basis this morning for you to build upon, that when we leave this meeting you will know exactly where you are.

In the beginning was the Word, and the Word was with God, and the Word was God. The same was in the beginning with God. All things were made by him; and without him was not any thing made that was made.

John 1:1-3

There we have the foundation of all things, which is the Word. It is a substance. It is a power. It is more than relationship. It is personality. It is a divine injunction to every soul that enters into this privilege to be born of this Word, to be created by this Word, to have a knowledge of this Word. What it means to us will be very important for us.

For remember, it is a substance, it is an evidence of things not seen. It bringeth about that which you cannot see. It brings forth that which is not there, and takes away that what is there, and substitutes it.

God took the Word and made the world of the things which did not appear. And we live in the world which was made by the Word of God, and it is inhabited by millions of people. And you say it is a substance. Jesus, the Word of God, made it of the things which did not appear.

And there is "not anything made that was made" that has not been made by that Word. And when we come to the truth of what that Word means, we shall be able not only to build but to know, not only to know, but to have. For if there is anything helping me today more than another, it is the fact I am living in facts, I am moving in facts, I am in the knowledge of the principles of the Most High.

God is making manifest His power. God is a reality and proving His mightiness in the midst of us. And as we open ourselves to divine revelation, and get rid of all things which are not of the Spirit, then we shall understand how mightily God can take us on in the Spirit, and move the things which are, and bring the things which are not, into prominence.

Oh, the riches, the depths of the wisdom of the Most High God! May this morning enlarge us. Jabus knew that there were divine principles that we need to know, and he says, "Enlarge me."

David knew that there was mightiness beyond and within, and he says, "Thou hast dealt bountifully with me," knowing that all the springs came from God that were in Him, which made His face to shine.

And God is an inward witness of a power, of a truth, of a revelation, of an inward presence, of a divine knowledge. He is! He is!

Then I must understand. I must clearly understand. I must have a basis of knowledge for everything that I say. We must, as preachers, never preach what we think. We must say what we know. Any man can think. You must be beyond the thinking. You must be in the teaching. You must have the knowledge.

And God wants to make us so in fidelity with Him that He unveils Himself. He rolls the clouds away, the mists disappear at His presence. He is almighty in His movements.

God has nothing small. He is all large, immensity of wisdom, unfolding the mysteries and the grandeur of His design of plan for humanity, that humanity may sink into insignificance, and the mightiness of the mighty power of God may move upon us till we are the sons of God with power, in revelation, and might, and strength in the knowledge of God.

Oh, this wonderful salvation! Now let us think about it, it is so beautiful. Seeing then that God took the Word—what was the Word? The Word was Jesus. The Word became flesh and dwelt among us. And we beheld and saw the glory of God.

I think John has a wonderful word on this which is to edify at this moment. Very powerful in its revelation to me so often as I gaze into the perfect law of liberty. Let me read you one verse, or perhaps more than one from the first epistle of John:

> That which was from the beginning, which we have heard, which we
> have seen with our eyes, which we have looked upon, and our hands
> have handled, of the Word of life; (For the life was manifested, and
> we have seen it, and bear witness, and show unto you that eternal
> life, which was with the Father, and was manifested unto us;) That
> which we have seen and heard declare we unto you, that ye also
> may have fellowship with us: and truly our fellowship is with the
> Father, and with His Son Jesus Christ.
>
> *1 John 1:1-3*

Oh, beloved, He is the Word! He is the principle of God. He is the revelation sent forth from God. All fullness dwelt in Him. This is a grand word, of His fullness we have all received, and grace for grace.

In weakness, strength. In poverty, wealth. Oh, brother, this Word! It is a flame of fire. It may burn in your bones. It may move in every tissue of your life. It may bring out of you so forcibly the plan and purpose and life of God, till you cease to be, for God has taken you.

It is a fact we may be taken, hallelujah! into all the knowledge of the wisdom of God. Then I want to build, if I am created anew, for it is a great creation. It took nine months to bring us forth into the world after we were conceived, but it only takes one moment to beget us as sons. The first formation was a long period of nine months. The second formation is a moment, is an act, is a faith, for "He that believeth hath." And as you receive Him, you are begotten, not made.

Oh, the fact that I am begotten again, wonderful! Begotten of the same seed that begot Him. Remember, as He was conceived in the womb by the Holy Ghost, so we were conceived the moment we believed, and became in a principle of the like-mindedness of an open door to become sons of God with promise.

And oh! how the whole creation groaneth for sonship! There is a word in Romans, I think it would help us this morning to read it. Some knowledge of sonship—it is a beautiful word. I have so often looked at it with pleasure, for it is such a pleasure to me to read the Word of God. Oh, the hidden treasures there are! What a feast to have the Word of God! "Man shall not live by bread alone, but by every Word of God."

How we need the Word! The Word is life. Now, think about this first word here. The 4th verse is very beautiful. I will read the 3rd and 4th:

> *Concerning his Son Jesus Christ our Lord, which was made of the seed of David according to the flesh; And declared to be the Son of God with power, according to the spirit of holiness, by the resurrection from the dead.*
>
> *Romans 1:3,4*

Oh, what a climax of beatitudes there is here! How beautiful! God, breathe upon us this morning this holy, inward way after His passion. Hear it. "Declared to be the Son of God with power."

Sons must have power. We must have power with God, power with man. We must be above all the world. We must have power over satan, power over the evils. I want you just this moment to think with me because it will help you with this thought.

You can never make evil pure. Anything which is evil never becomes pure in that sense. There is no such a thing as ever creating impurity into purity. The carnal mind is never subject to the will of God, and cannot be. There is only one thing. It must be destroyed.

But I want you to go with me to when God cast out that which was not pure. I want you to think about satan in the glory with all the chances, and nothing spoiled him but his pride. And pride is an awful thing. Pride in the heart, thinking we are something when we are nothing. Building up a human constitution out of our own.

Oh, yes, it is true the devil is ever trying to make you think what you are. You never find God doing it. It is always satan who comes on and says, "What a wonderful address you gave! How wonderful he did that, and how wonderful he prayed, and sung that song." It is all of the devil. There is not an atom of God in it, not from beginning to end.

And if we only knew how much we could preach better, if we only would not miss the revelation. And Paul, in order that he might never miss the revelation, said, "Therefore I have never ceased, I have kept that."

Oh, the vision is so needy today, more needy than anything that man should have the visions of God. The people have always perished when there has been no vision. God wants us to have visions, and revelations, and manifestations.

You cannot have the Holy Ghost without having manifestations. You cannot have the Holy Ghost without having revelations. You cannot have the Holy Ghost without being turned into another nature. It was the only credential so Joshua and Caleb could enter the land because they were of another spirit.

And we must live in an unction, in a power, in a transformation, and a divine attainment where we cease to be, where God becomes enthroned so richly.

TONGUES AND INTERPRETATION: "It is He! He came forth, emptied Himself of all, but love brought to us the grace, and then offered by Himself to purge us that we might be entire and free from all things. That we should see Him who was invisible, and changed by the power which is divine, and be lost to everything but the immensity of the mightiness of a God-likeness, for we must be in the world sons of God with promise."

We must be, we must be! We must not say it is not for me. Oh no, we must say it is for us. And God cast satan out. Oh, I do thank God for that. Yes, beloved, but God could not have cast him out if he had even been equal of power. I tell you, beloved, we can never bind the strong man till we are in the place of binding.

Thank God, satan had to come out. Yes, and how did he come out? By the Word of His power. And beloved, if we get to know and understand the principles of our inheritance by faith, we shall find out satan will always be cast out by the same power that cast him out in the beginning. He will be cast out to the end because satan has not become more holy but more vile.

If you think about the last day upon the earth, you will find out that the greatest war—not Armageddon, the war beyond that—will be betwixt the hosts of satan and the hosts of God. And how will it take place? With swords, dynamite, or any other human power? No, by the brightness of His presence, the holiness of His holiness, the purity of His purity, where darkness cannot remain, where sin cannot stand, where only holiness, purity will remain. All else will flee from the presence of God into the abyss forever.

And God has saved us with this Word of power over the powers of sin. I know there is a teaching and a need of teaching of the personality of the presence of the fidelity of the Word of God with power. And we need to eat and drink of this Word. We need to feed upon it in our hearts. We need that holy revelation that ought always to take away the mists from our eyes and reveal Him.

Remember beloved, don't forget that every day must be a day of advancement. If you have not made any advancement since yesterday, in a measure you are a backslider. There is only one way for you between Calvary and the glory, and it is forward. It is every day forward. It is no day back. It is advancement with God. It is cooperation with Him in the Spirit.

Beloved, we must see these things, because if we live on the same plane, day after day, the vision is stale, the principles lose their earnestness. But we must be like those who are catching the vision of the Master day by day. And we must make inroads into every passion that would interfere, and bring everything to the slaughter that is not holy. For God would have us in these days to know that He wishes to seat us on High. Don't forget it.

The principles remain with us if we will only obey, to seat us on High, hallelujah! And let us still go on building because we must build this morning. We must know our foundation. We must be able to take the Word of God, and so make it clear to people because we shall be confronted with evil powers.

I am continually confronted with things which God must clear away. Every day something comes before me that has to be dealt with on these lines. For instance, when I was at Cazadero seven or eight years ago, amongst the first people who came to me in those meetings, was a man who was stone deaf. And every time we had the meeting—suppose I was rising up to say a few words, this man would take his chair from off the ordinary row and place it right in front of me. And the devil used to say, "Now, you are done." I said, "No, I am not done. It is finished."

The man was as deaf as possible for three weeks. And then in the meeting, as we were singing about three weeks afterward, this man became tremendously disturbed as though in a storm. He looked in every direction, and then he became as one who had almost lost his mind.

And then he took a leap. He started on the run and went out amongst the people, and right up one of the hills. When he got about 60 yards away he heard singing. And the Lord said, "Thy ears are open."

And he came back, and we were still singing. That stopped our singing. And then he told us that when his ears were opened, he could not understand what it was. There was such a tremendous noise he could not understand it whatever. He thought something had happened to the world, and so he ran out of the whole thing. Then when he got away he heard singing.

Oh, the devil said for three weeks, "You cannot do it." I said, "It is done!" As though God would ever forget! As though God could forget! As if it were possible for God to ever ignore our prayers!

The most trying time is the most helpful time. Most preachers say something about Daniel, and about the Hebrew children, and especially about Moses when he was in a tried corner. Beloved, if you read the Scriptures you will never find anything about the easy time. All the glories come out of hard times.

And if you are really reconstructed it will be in a hard time, it won't be in a singing meeting, but at a time when you think all things are dried up, when you think there is no hope for you, and you have passed everything, then that is the time that God makes the man, when tried by fire, that God purges you, takes the dross away, and brings forth the pure gold. Only melted gold is minted. Only moistened clay receives the mold.

Only softened wax receives the seal. Only broken, contrite hearts receive the mark as the Potter turns us on His wheel, shaped and burnt to take and keep the heavenly mold, the stamp of God's pure gold.

We must have the stamp of our blessed Lord who was marred more than any man. And when He touched human weakness it was reconstructed. He spoke out of the depths of trial and mockery, and became the initiative of a world's redemption. Never man spake like He spake! He was full of order and made all things move till they said, We never saw it on this like.

He was truly the Son of God with power, with blessing, with life, with maturity, that He could take the weakest and make them into strong and strength.

God is here this morning in power, in blessing, in might, and saying to thee, my brother, and to you, my sister, "What is it? What is thy request?"

Oh, He is so precious! He never fails! He is so wonderful! He always touches the needy place. He is so gentle. He never breaks the bruised reed. He is so rich in His mighty benevolence that He makes the smoking flax to flame.

May God move us this morning to see that He must have out of us choice. Oh, how precious He is! There is no word so precious to me as when He said, "I have desired to eat this with you before I suffer."

Oh, that lovely, benevolent, wonderful Jesus! Oh, before the garden experience, with the knowledge of it before the cross, and Gethsemane, there that love of Jesus, that holy Jesus, could say, with desire! It was the joy that was set before Him. Shall it be missed? Is it possible for it to be missed? That joy that was set before Him of making us fully matured saints of God, with power over the powers of the enemy, filled with the might of His Spirit.

Surely this is our God, for there are no other God answers like this. Beloved, let me entreat you this morning to pay any price. Never mind what it costs, it is worth it all to have His smile, to have His presence. Nay verily, more than that, to have the same desire that He had to win others for Him.

When I see His great desire to win me, I say, "Lord, remold me like that. Make me have the desire of salvation for others at any cost." Thank God He went through. He did not look back. He went right on.

Oh, you never need to be afraid of joining yourself to this Nazarene, for He is always a King. When He was dying He was a King. Yes, if ever any man spoke in tongues, Jesus spoke in tongues, for there was no interpretation. And if any man ever spoke truth He spoke the truth when He said, "It is finished."

Thank God it is finished. And I know, because it is finished, everything is mine. Thank God, everything is mine, things in heaven, things in earth, things under the earth. He is all power over all. He is in all. He is through all. Thank God He is for all.

And I say to you without contradiction, that Jesus has so much more for you than you have any conception. Just as the two sons of Zebedee, did they know what they asked? Certainly, they had no conception of their asking.

Jesus said, "Are ye able to drink of the cup that I shall drink of and to be baptized with the baptism that I am baptized with? They say unto Him, 'We are able'." Were they able? No, but it was their heart. Have a big heart! Have a big yes! Have a big "I will!" Have a great desire though you are blind to what is to follow.

And they wondered what He had. I believe that all believers want the same. Did they drink? Yes, He said they would. Did they see His baptism? Yes, He said they would. But they had no idea what it meant, what the cup was.

But the cup was drunk to the dregs. Yes, His cup was different. But because of His cup, our cup runneth over. Oh, surely goodness and mercy shall follow thee. Thy cup shall run over.

There may be many cups before the cup is full. But oh, hallelujah, any way, only let it be His will and His way, not my way. Oh, for His way only, and His plan, His will only.

I feel we have gotten very little out of the subject, but oh, what shall we say? What are we going to do? Brothers, let the mantle fall from Him on you today. "If thou see me when I go, it shall be." And Elisha kept his eye on Elijah. The mantle is to fall, my brother; the mantle of power, the mantle of blessing.

And I ask you today, seeing that you have this spiritual revelation in the body, in the earthly tabernacle, what are you going to do? If the body is yielded sufficiently till it becomes perfectly the temple of the Spirit, then the fullness will flow, and the life shall be yielded to you, given to you as you need.

May God mold us all to believe it is possible this morning not only for the rivers but the mightiness of the expansiveness of that mighty ocean of His to flow through us.

You do as you are led to do. The altar rail is before you. No pressure ought to be needed for you as you see your need before God, and know He is here to supply your need. Wherefore, why should we have to be entreated to seek the best of all when God is waiting to give without measure to each and all.

Do as the Lord leads you, and we will be still before Him to let Him direct you in whatever way.

Glad Tidings Tabernacle and Bible Training School
San Francisco, California

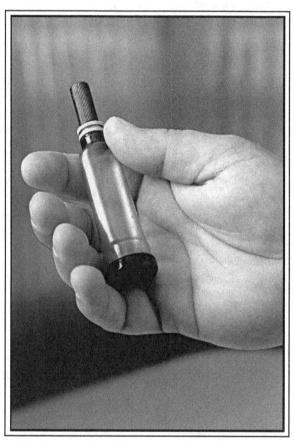

The vial of oil used for healing that Wigglesworth
regularly carried with him

FAITH THAT LEADS TO
THE TREASURES OF GOD
August 3, 1922

I believe the Lord would be magnified and be pleased if we are to continue our subject we had yesterday morning from the 11th chapter of Hebrews. I will read from the first verse:

Now faith is the substance of things hoped for, the evidence of things not seen. For by it the elders obtained a good report. Through faith we understand that the worlds were framed by the word of God, so that things which are seen were not made of things which do appear. By faith Abel offered unto God a more excellent sacrifice than Cain, by which he obtained witness that he was righteous, God testifying of his gifts: and by it he being dead yet speaketh. By faith Enoch was translated that he should not see death; and was not found, because God had translated him: for before his translation he had this testimony, that he pleased God. But without faith it is impossible to please him: for he that cometh to God must believe that he is, and that he is a rewarder of them that diligently seek him. By faith Noah, being warned of God of things not seen as yet, moved with fear, prepared an ark to the saving of his house; by the which he condemned the world, and became heir of the righteousness which is by faith. By faith Abraham, when he was called to go out into a place which he should after receive for an inheritance, obeyed; and he went out, not knowing whither he went. By faith he sojourned in the land of promise, as in a strange country, dwelling in tabernacles with Isaac and Jacob, the heirs with him of the same promise: For he looked for a city which hath foundations, whose builder and maker is God.

Hebrews 11:1-10

I believe that there is only one way to all the treasures of God, and it is the way of faith. There is only one principle underlying all the attributes and all the beatitudes of the mighty ascension into the glories of Christ, and it is by faith. All the promises are Yea and Amen to them who believe.

And God wants this morning, by His own way—for He has a way and it never comes human, it always comes on divine principles, you cannot know God by nature. You get to know God by an open door of grace.

He has made a way. It is a beautiful way that all His saints can enter in by that way and find rest. The way is the way of faith. There isn't any other way. If you climb up any other way, you cannot work it out.

There [are] several things that are coming before me from time to time, and I find that it is all a failure without its base is right on the rock Christ Jesus. He is the only way, the truth, and the life. But praise God, He is the truth, He is the life, and His Word is Spirit and life-giving. And when we understand it in its true order to us we find that it is not only the Word of life but it quickeneth, it openeth, it filleth, it moveth, it changeth, and it brings us into a place where we dare to say, Amen!

You know, beloved, there is a lot in an Amen. You know you never get but still you have an Amen inside. There was such a difference between Zacharias and Mary. I find you can have zeal without faith. And I find you can have any amount of things without faith.

As I looked into the 12th chapter of the Acts of the Apostles, I find that the people who were waiting all night praying for Peter to come out of prison had zeal but they had not faith. They were so zealous that they even gave themselves only to eat the unleavened bread, and went to prayer. And it seemed all the time that there was much that could be commended to us all this morning, but there was one thing missing. It was faith. You will find that Rhoda had more faith than all the rest of them. When the knock came at the door, she ran to it and the moment she heard Peter's voice she ran back again with joy, saying, "Peter stood before the gate."

And all the people said, "You are mad. It isn't so." And she made mention of what she saw. There was no faith at all. But they said, "Well, God has perhaps sent an angel." But Rhoda said, "It is Peter." And Peter continued knocking. And they went and found it was so. They had zeal but no faith. And I believe there is quite a difference.

God wants to bring us into an activity where we shall in a living way take hold of God on the lines of solidity, that which rests and sees the plan of God always.

Zacharias and Elizabeth surely wanted a son, but even when the angel came and told Zacharias he was full of unbelief. And the angel said, "Because thou hast not believed, thou shalt be dumb."

But look at Mary. When the angel came to Mary, Mary said, "...be it unto me according to thy word." And it was the beginning of the Amen, and the presentation of the Amen was when she nursed Jesus.

Believe that there can be a real Amen in your life that can come to pass. And God wants us with the Amen that never knows anything else than Amen, an inward Amen, a mighty moving Amen, a God-likeness Amen. That which says, "It is," because God has spoken. It cannot be otherwise. It is impossible to be otherwise.

Beloved, I see all the plan of life where God comes in and vindicates His power, makes His presence felt. It is not by crying, nor groaning. It is because we believe. And yet, I have nothing to say about it. Sometimes it takes God a long time to bring us through the groaning, crying, before we can believe.

I know this as clearly as anything, that no man in this place can change God. You cannot change Him. There is a word in Finney's lectures which is very good, and it says, "Can a man who is full of sin and all kinds of ruin in his life change God when he comes out to pray?" No, it is impossible. But as this man labors in prayer, and groans, and travails, because his tremendous sin is weighing him down, he becomes broken in the presence of God, and when properly melted in the perfect harmony with the divine plan of God, then God can work in that clay. He could not before.

Prayer changes hearts but it never changes God. God is the same today and forever, full of love, full of entreaty, full of helpfulness. Always in the presence of God as you come you have what you come for. You take it away. You can use it at your disposal.

And there is nothing you can find in the Scriptures where God ever charges you for what you have done with what He has given you. God upbraids no man, but you can come and come again, and God is willing to give if you believe.

TONGUES AND INTERPRETATION: "It is the living God. It is the God of power who changes things, changes us. It is He Who has formed us, not we ourselves, and transformed us because it is He Who comes in and makes the vessel ready for the immensity of its power working through us, transforming us into His will, His plan, for He delighteth in us."

God delighteth in us. When a man's ways please the Lord, then He makes all things to move accordingly.

Now we come to the Word, this blessed Word, this holy Word. I want to go to the 5th verse of the 11th [chapter] of Hebrews. We were dealing with the two first verses yesterday.

> By faith Enoch was translated that he should not see death; and was not found, because God had translated him: for before his translation he had this testimony, that he pleased God.
>
> *Hebrews 11:5*

When I was in Sweden, the Lord worked mightily there in a very blessed way—after one or two addresses the leaders called me and they said, "We have heard very strange things about you, and we would like to know whether they are true because we can see the doors are opening to you. We can see that God is with you, and God is moving, and we know that it will be a great blessing to Sweden."

"Well," I said, "what is it?" "Well," they said, "we have heard from good authority that you preach that you have the resurrection body."

When I was in France I had an interpreter that believed this thing, and I found out after I had preached once or twice through the interpreter that she gave her own expressions. And of course I did not know but I said, "Nevertheless, I will tell you what I really believe. If I had the testimony of Enoch I should be off. I would like it and I would like to go. Evidently there is no one in Sweden who has it or they would be off, because the moment Enoch had the testimony to please God, off he went."

I pray that God will so quicken our faith for we have a far way to go maybe before we are ready. It was in the mind of God, translation. But remember translation comes on the lines of holy obedience and walk with pleasure with a perfectness of God. Walking together with God in the Spirit. Some others have had touches of it. It is lovely, it is delightful to think about those moments as we have walked with God and had communion with Him, when our words were lifted, and we were not made to make them, but God made them.

Oh, that smile of divine communication which is truly of God, where we speak to Him in the Spirit, and where the Spirit lifts and lifts and lifts, and takes us in. Oh, beloved, there is a place of God where God can bring us in, and I pray that God by His Spirit, may move us so we will strive to be where Enoch was as he walked with God.

As Paul divinely puts it by the Spirit, I don't believe that any person in this place hasn't an open door into everything that is in the Scriptures. I believe the Scriptures are for us. And in order that we may apply our hearts to understand the truth I say, Oh, for an inroad of the mighty revolution of the human heart to break it so that God can plan afresh and make all within us say, Amen! What a blessed experience it is, truly.

There are two kinds of faith that God wants to let us see. I am not speaking about natural things this morning but divine things. There is a natural faith and there is a saving faith. The saving faith is the gift of God. All people are born with the natural faith. But this supernatural faith is the gift of God.

And yet there are limitations in this faith. But faith which has no limitation in God, comes to us this morning in the 26th chapter of the Acts of the apostles. This is a very wonderful chapter. I want to define, or express, or bring into prominence this morning the difference between the natural faith and this faith that I am going to read about, beginning at the 16th verse:

> *But rise, and stand upon thy feet: for I have appeared unto thee for this purpose, to make thee a minister and a witness both of these things which thou hast seen, and of those things in the which I will appear unto thee; Delivering thee from the people, and from the Gentiles, unto whom now I send thee, To open their eyes, and to turn them from darkness to light, and from the power of Satan unto God, that they may receive forgiveness of sins, and inheritance among them which are sanctified by faith that is in me.*
>
> *Acts 26:16-18*

Is that the faith of Paul? No, it is the faith which the Holy Ghost is giving. We may have very much of revelation of a divine plan of God through the gifts in the Lord's order, when He speaks to me I will open out on the gifts.

But beloved, I see here just a touch of the line of the gifts, where Paul, through the revelation, and through the open door that was given to him on the way to Damascus, saw he had the faith of salvation. Then I notice as Ananias laid his hands upon him, there came a power, the promise of the Holy Ghost, and filled this body.

And then I notice in that order of the Spirit, he walked in the comfort of the Holy Ghost, which is a wonderful comfort. Oh, tell me if you can, is there anything to compare to that which Jesus said, when He comes "...he shall teach you all things, and bring all things to your remembrance..." (John 14:26). Surely this is a Comforter. Surely He is the Comforter who can bring to our memory, to our mind, all the things that He said.

And all the way He worked is the divine plan of the Spirit to reveal unto us till every one of us, without exception, tastes of this angelic mighty touch of the heavenly as He moves upon us.

Oh, beloved, the baptism of the Holy Ghost is the essential mighty touch of revelation of the wonders, for God the Holy Ghost has no limitations on these lines. But when the soul is ready to enter into His life, there is a breaking up of fallow ground and a moving of the mists away, bringing us into the perfect day of the light of God.

And I say that Paul was moved upon by this power, and yet Jesus said unto him, "As you go you will be changed, and in the changing I will take you from revelation to revelation, open door to open door and the accomplishment will be as My faith is committed unto thee."

Oh, hallelujah, there is saving faith. There is the gift of faith. It is the faith of Jesus which brings to us as we press in and on with God, a place where we can always know it is God.

I want just to put before you this difference between our faith and the faith of Jesus. Our faith comes to an end. Most people in this place have come to a place where they have said, "Lord, I can go no further. I have gone so far, now I can go no further. I have used all the faith I have, and I have just to stop now and wait."

Well, brother, thank God that we have this faith. But there is another faith. I remember one day being in Lancashire, and going around to see some sick people. I was taken into a house where there was a young woman lying on her bed, a very helpless case. It was a case where the reason had gone, and many things were manifested there which were satanic, and I knew it.

She was only a young woman, a beautiful child. Then the husband, quite a young man, came in with a baby and he leaned over to kiss the wife. The moment he did she threw herself over on the other side of the bed, just as a lunatic would do, with no consciousness of the presence of the husband.

That was very heart-breaking. And then he took the baby and pressed the baby's lips to the mother. Again another wild kind of thing happened. So he said to a sister who was attending her, "Have you anybody to help?" "Oh," they said, "we have had everything."

But I said, "Have you no spiritual help?" And her husband stormed out and said, "Help? You think that we believe in God after we have had seven weeks of no sleep, of maniac conditions? You think that we believe God? You are mistaken. You have come to the wrong house."

And then a young woman about 18 or so just grinned at me and passed out of the door, and that finished the whole business. That brought me to a place of compassion for this woman that something had to be done, did not matter what it was.

And then with my faith—oh, thank God for the faith. I began to penetrate the heavens, and I was soon out of that house I will tell you, for I never saw a man get anything from God who prayed on the earth. If you get anything from God you will have to pray into heaven for it is all there. If you are living on the earth and expect things from heaven it will never come. If you want to touch the ideal you must live in ideal principles.

And as I saw in the presence of God the limitations of my faith, there came another faith, a faith that could not be denied, a faith that took the promise, a faith that believed God's Word. And I came from that presence back again to earth, but not the same man, under the same condition confronting me but in the name of Jesus, with a faith that could shake hell and move anything else.

I said, "Come out of her in the name of Jesus!" And she rolled over and fell asleep and wakened in 14 hours, perfectly sane and perfectly whole. Oh, there is faith. The faith that is in me. And Jesus wants to bring us all this morning into a place in line with God where we cease to be, for God must have the right of way, of thought, of purpose. God must have the way.

Beloved, I say there is a process on this line. Enoch walked with God. That must have been all these hundreds of years as he was penetrating, and going through, and laying hold, and believing, and seeing that he had got-ten to such cooperation and touch with God that things moved on earth, and was moving toward heaven. And surely God came for the last time.

It was not possible for him to stop any longer. Oh, hallelujah! And I believe that God this morning wants to so bring all of us into line with His will that we may see signs, and wonders, and divers miracles and gifts of the Holy Ghost. For this is a wonderful day, the day of the Holy Ghost. It is a blessed day. If you would ask me any time, "When would you have liked to come to earth?" Just now! Oh, yes, it suits me beautifully to know that the Holy Ghost can fill the body. Just to be a temple of the Spirit! Just to manifest the glory of God! Brother, it is truly an ideal summit, and everyone can reach out their hand and God will take and lift us on.

For the heart that is longing this morning, God makes the longing cry. Sometimes we have an idea that there is some specialty in us that does it. No, beloved. If you have anything at all worth having it is because God has love to give you.

According to the 15th chapter of First Corinthians everybody who dies—I see there is a place where they have fallen short somehow to me. It can never appear as the right thing, as it is sown in dishonor. It seems to be truly that God will raise it in power, the same power God would raise it in is the power that God wants to keep us in, so as we should not be sown in dishonor.

I truly say that there is a plan of God for this purpose, of this life. Enoch walked with God. God wants to raise the conditions of saints to walk with Him, and talk with Him. I don't want to build anything about myself, but it is truly true if you found me outside of conversation with man, I am in conversation with God.

One thing God has given to me from my youth up, and I am so thankful, God has never given me a taste or a relish for any book but the Bible. And I can say before God, I have never read a book but the Bible, so I know nothing about books. As I have peeped into books I have seen in them just one thing that good people said, "Well, that is a good book." Oh, but how much better to get the Book of books which contains nothing but God. If a book is commended because it has something about God in it, how much more shall the Word of God be the food of the soul, the strengthening of the believer, and the building up of the human order of character with God, so that all the time he is being changed by the Spirit of the Lord from one state of glory into another.

This is the ideal principle of God. I have a word to say about those who have gone, because Paul says, "It is better to go than to stop." But oh, I am looking forward, and hasting unto, and believing the fact that He is coming again.

And this hope in me brings me to the same place as the man of faith who looked for a city which human hands had not made. There is a city which human hands have not made, and by faith we have a right to claim our position right along as we go, and to these glorious positions.

I will turn now from this fifth verse to the sixth, also a beautiful verse of Hebrews 11:

But without faith it is impossible to please him: for he that cometh to God must believe that he is, and that he is a rewarder of them that diligently seek him.

Hebrews 11:6

I often think that we make great failures on this line because of an imperfect understanding of His Word. I can see it is impossible to please God on any lines but faith, for everything which is not of faith is sin.

So God wants us all to see this morning the plan of faith is the ideal and principle of God. And when I remember and keep in my thoughts these beautiful words in the 12th chapter of this same epistle, it is wonderful as I read this second verse:

Looking unto Jesus the author and finisher of our faith....

Hebrews 12:2

He is the author of faith. Jesus became the author of faith. God worked the plan through Him by forming the worlds, making everything that there was by the Word of His power. Jesus was the Word, Christ. God so manifested this power in the world, forming the worlds by the word of Jesus.

I see that on this divine line of principle of God, God hath chosen Him and ordained Him, and clothed Him, and made Him greater than all because of one principle, and on this principle only. Because of the joy, it was the love of God that gave. It was the joy of the Lord to save.

And because of this exceeding, abundant joy of saving the whole world, He became the author of a living faith. And everyone in this place is changed by this faith from grace to grace. We become divine inheritances of the promises, and we become the substance. We can become all and in all.

One ideal only, God is working in this, this holy principle of faith. It is divine.

TONGUES AND INTERPRETATION: "It is God installed through the flesh, quickened by His Spirit, molded by His will, till it is so in order, till God's Son could not come without we went for His life is in us."

Thank God for that interpretation. God's Son, this life, this faith, could not move from the glory without I move from the earth. And right in the heaven we should meet.

This faith, this principle, this life, this inheritance, this truth, this eternal power working in us mightily by His Spirit! Oh, thank God for His Word! Live it, moved by His Word.

We shall become flat, and anemic, and helpless without this Word, dormant and so helpless to take hold. You are not any good for anything apart from the Word. The Word is everything. The Word has to become everything. When the heavens and the earth are melted away then we shall be as bright, and brighter than the day, and going on to be consistent because of the Word of God.

Oh, when we know it is quick, and powerful, and sharper than any two-edged sword, dividing asunder soul and spirit, joints and marrow, and thoughts of the heart! God's Word is like a sword piercing through. Who could have a stiff knee if they believed in that Word?

The Word is so divinely appointed for us. Think about it. How it severs the soul and the spirit! Take it in. Think it out. Work it out. It is divine. See it, truth.

The soul which has all the animal, all the carnal, all the selfishness, all the evil things, thank God for the truth to the Word, that the soul will never inherit that place. The soul must go from whence it came. It is earthly, sensual. But the two-edged sword divides it so it shall have no power. And over it, ruling it, controlling it, bringing it always to death, is the Spirit of the life of Jesus.

Jesus poured out His soul unto death. Flesh and blood shall not inherit the kingdom of heaven. So I see it is necessary for us to have the Word of God piercing even to dividing asunder soul and spirit.

Then I notice the joints and marrow must have the Word of God to quicken the very marrow. Oh, how many people in Australia came to me with double-curvature of the spine, and instantly they were healed, and made straight as I put hands upon them. But no man is able, but the divine Son of God and His power moved upon these curvatures of the spine, and straightened them. Oh, the mighty power of the Word of God!

God must have us in these days so separated on every line as we proceed on the lines of God, and see that the Word of God must bring forth. As it destroys it brings forth. You can never live if you have never been dead. You must die if you want to live. It was the very death of Jesus that raised Him to the highest height of glory.

Every death-likeness is a likeness to the Son of God. And all the time the Word of God must quicken, flow through, and move upon us till these ideals are in us, till we move in them, live in them.

TONGUES AND INTERPRETATION: "The living God is lifting thee out of thyself into Himself."

We must be taken out of the ordinary. We must be brought into the extraordinary. We must live in a glorious position, over the flesh and the devil, and everything of the world. God has ordained us, clothed us within, and manifested upon us His glory that we may be the sons with promise, of Son-likeness to Him.

Oh, what an ideal! What a Savior! What an ideal Savior! And to be like Him! Oh, yes, we can be like Him. This is the ideal principle, God to make us like Him!

Then I see another truth. He that cometh to God—how do you come to God? Where is God? Is He in the ceiling? In the elements? Is He in the air? In the wind? Where is God? He that cometh to God—where is He? God is in you. Oh, hallelujah! And you will find the Spirit of the living God in you, which is the prayer circle, which is the lifting power, which is the revelation element, which is the divine power which lifts you.

He that cometh to God is. He is already in the place where the Holy Ghost takes the prayers and swings them out according to the mind of the Spirit. For who hath known the mind of Christ, or who is able to make intercession but the mind of the Spirit of the living God. He maketh intercession. Where is He? He is in us.

Oh, this baptism of the Holy Ghost is an inward presence of the personality of God, which lifts, prays, takes hold, lives in, with a tranquility of peace and power that rests and says, "It is all right."

God answers prayer because the Holy Ghost prays and your advocate is Jesus, and the Father the Judge of all. There He is. Is it possible for any prayer to be missed on those lines? Let us be sure that we are in this place this morning.

"He that cometh to God must believe that He is, and that He is a rewarder of them that diligently seek Him." You must believe that God is. You cannot help it. You must believe He is already in the temple.

But some people have not yet entered into the experience because they have never come out. But God said to Abraham, "Come out, Come out." And if you have never known the voice of God to come out, you may be a long time in the wilderness before you come in.

Now look at the ridiculousness of Abraham—that is the human side. Look at it in verse 8: "By faith Abraham, when he was called to go out into a place which he should after receive for an inheritance, obeyed; and he went out..." (Heb. 11:8). What a silly man he was!

"...not knowing whither he went." Why, that was the very secret of power. Everything was there. If there is anything that I know which is worth knowing, it is that which I don't know about God which He is always making me to know.

There is something about being after God's mind till we will be all the time what He wants us to be. God has ordered it so. God has planned it so. God wills it. So God has no other method or plan of saving ruined man except by man.

And when man remains in the place which God has called him out, so that he can be a perfect man, substitute of God's plan for the man, then the man will surely reach the attitude where God has said, Come out, for I have a place for thee and thou canst never reach the place without Me. But I am willing that thou shouldst be for Me that I may be for thee.

Oh, this God of grace! Oh, this willingness for God to let us see His face! Oh, this longing of my soul which cannot be satisfied without more of God! Oh, it is this, more of God I want! I feel that I am the youngest man in the world.

Without God does something I should be an awful failure. But surely He will do it. He has brought us in that He might take us out. And God will never leave us in an unfinished plane.

It is all divine order. As surely as Jesus came, it is divine order that I should come at this time to San Francisco. There is nothing wrong in the plan of God. It is all in perfect order. To think that God can make a mistake is the biggest blunder that a man makes in his life. God makes no mistakes. But when we are in the will of God the plan works out admirably because it is divine, thought out by the almightiness of God.

Oh, beloved, have you come out yet? You say, "Out of what?" Out of that you know you didn't want to be in. Why should I answer your questions when you can answer them yourselves? It would be a waste of time. No need of going on that line.

But God knows where you are and where you ought to be. Many of you heard the voice of God long ago, but still you have not obeyed. Will you come out? God says, "Come out!" But you say, "Where shall I go to? Where shall I come out?" Come out into God! Unto God! Oh, hallelujah!

I would like to say so many more things to you this morning, but I think it is just about time to come out. It is such a mistake to hold on, hearing His voice and not obeying. But oh, when we obey, it is so sweet when we obey! So I will cease at this time because God has something better probably teaching you in the Spirit as you obey His call, obey His "Come out."

God has something better for you than I can tell you. Oh, I say to you, Come out, and I will leave you to either sit still or come out. Amen!

Message given at Glad Tidings Tabernacle and Bible Training School
San Francisco, California

THE GOD KIND OF FAITH

September 16, 1922

Read Hebrews 11:1-11. I believe that there is only one way to all the treasures of God, and that is the way of faith. By faith and faith alone do we enter into a knowledge of the attributes so that we can become partakers of the beatitudes, and participate in the glories of our ascended Lord. All His promises are Yea and Amen to them who believe.

God would have us come to Him by His own way. That is through the open door of grace. A way has been made. It is a beautiful way, and all His saints can enter in by this way and find rest. God has prescribed that the just shall live by faith. I find that all is a failure that has not its base on the rock Christ Jesus. He is the only way, the truth, and the life. The way of faith is the Christ way, receiving Him in His fullness and walking in Him; receiving His quickening life that filleth, moveth, and changeth us, bringing us to a place where there is always an Amen in our hearts to all the will of God.

Let us examine this fifth verse of Hebrews 11: "By faith Enoch was translated that he should not see death; and was not found, because God had translated him: for before his translation he had this testimony, that he pleased God."

When I was in Sweden, the Lord worked mightily. After one or two addresses the leaders called me and said, "We have heard very strange things about you, and we would like to know if they are true. We can see that God is with you, and that God is moving, and we know that it will be a great blessing to Sweden."

"Well," I said, "what is it?"

"Well," they said, "we have heard from good authority that you preach that you have the resurrection body." When I was in France I had an interpreter that believed this thing, and I found out after I had preached once or twice through the interpreter that she gave her own expressions. And of course I did not know. I said to these brethren, "I tell you what my personal convictions are. I believe that if I had the testimony of Enoch I should be off. I believe that the moment Enoch had the testimony that he pleased God, off he went."

I pray that God will so quicken our faith, for translation is in the mind of God; but remember that translation comes on the line of holy obedience and a walk that is pleasing to God. This was true of Enoch. And I believe that we must have a like walk with God in the Spirit, having communion with Him, living under His divine smile, and I pray that God by His Spirit may so move us that we will be where Enoch was when he walked with God.

There are two kinds of faith. There is the natural faith. But the supernatural faith is the gift of God. In Acts 26:18, Paul is telling Agrippa of what the Lord said to him in commissioning him,

> *To open their eyes, and to turn them from darkness to light, and from the power of Satan unto God, that they may receive forgiveness of sins, and inheritance among them which are sanctified by faith that is in me.*
>
> *Acts 26:18*

Is that the faith of Paul? No, it is the faith that the Holy Ghost is giving. It is the faith that He brings to us as we press in and on with God. I want to put before you this difference between our faith and the faith of Jesus. Our faith comes to an end. Most people in this place have come to where they have said, "Lord, I can go no further. I have gone so far and I can go no further. I have used all the faith I have, and I have just to stop now and wait."

I remember one day being in Lancashire, and going round to see some sick people. I was taken into a house where there was a young woman lying on a bed, a very helpless case. The reason had gone, and many things were manifested there which were satanic and I knew it. She was only a young woman, a beautiful child. The husband, quite a young man, came in with the baby, and he leaned over to kiss the wife. The moment he did, she threw herself over on the other side, just as a lunatic would do. That was very heartbreaking. Then he took the baby and pressed the baby's lips to the mother. Again another wild kind of thing happened. I asked one who was attending her, "Have you anybody to help?" "Oh," they said, "We have had everything." "But," I said, "have you no spiritual help?" Her husband stormed out and said, "Help? You think that we believe in God after we have had seven weeks of no sleep and maniac conditions. You think that we believe God. You are mistaken. You have come to the wrong house."

Then a young woman of about 18 or so just grinned at me and passed out of the door, and that finished the whole business. That brought me to a place of compassion for the woman that something had to be done, no matter what it was. Then with my faith I began to penetrate the heavens, and I was soon out of that house I will tell you, for I never saw a man get anything from God who prayed on the earth. If you get anything from God you will have to pray into heaven for it is all there. If you are living in the earth realm and expect things from heaven, they will never come. And as I saw in the presence of God the limitations of my faith, there came another faith, a faith that could not be denied, a faith that took the promise, a faith that believed God's Word. And I came from that presence back again to earth, but not the same man under the conditions confronting me. God gave a faith that could shake hell and anything else.

I said, "Come out of her in the name of Jesus!" And she rolled over and fell asleep and wakened in 14 hours perfectly sane and perfectly whole.

There is a process on this line. Enoch walked with God. That must have been all those years as he was penetrating, and going through, and laying hold, and believing and seeing and getting into such close cooperation and touch with God that things moved on earth and he began to move toward heaven. At last it was not possible for him to stop any longer. Oh, hallelujah!

In the 15th chapter of First Corinthians we read of the body being "sown with dishonor," to be raised in power. It seems to me that as we are looking for translation that the Lord would have us know something of that power now, and would have us kept in that power, so that we should not be sown in dishonor.

Enoch walked with God. God wants to raise the condition of saints so that they walk with Him and talk with Him. I don't want to build anything round myself, but it is true that if you find me outside of conversation with man, you will find me in conversation with God.

There in one thing that God has given me from my youth up, a taste and relish for my Bible. I can say before God, I have never read a book but my Bible, so I know nothing about books. It seems better to me to get the Book of books for food for your soul, for the strengthening of your faith and the building up of your character in God, so that all the time you are being changed and made meet to walk with God.

> ...without faith it is impossible to please him: for he that cometh to God must believe that he is, and that he is a rewarder of them that diligently seek him.
>
> *Hebrews 11:6*

I can see that it is impossible to please Him on any lines but faith, for everything that is not of faith is sin. God wants us to see that the plan of faith is the ideal and principle of God. In this connection I love to keep in my thoughts the beautiful words in the second verse of the twelfth chapter of Hebrews: "Looking unto Jesus the author and finisher of our faith...." He is the author of faith. God worked through Him for the forming of the worlds. All things were made by Him and without Him was not anything made that was made. And because of the exceeding abundant joy of providing for us so great salvation, He became the author of a living faith. And through this principle of living faith, looking unto Him who is the author and finisher of our faith, we are changed into the same image from glory to glory, even by the Spirit of the Lord.

God has something better for you than you have ever had in the past. Come out into all the fullness of faith and power and life and victory that He is willing to provide, as you forget the things of the past, and press right on for the prize of His calling in Christ Jesus.

Published in *The Pentecostal Evangel*

LEARNING TO TRUST
A WONDERFUL GOD

December 9, 1922

For verily I say unto you, That whosoever shall say unto this mountain, Be thou removed, and be thou cast into the sea; and shall not doubt in his heart, but shall believe that those things which he saith shall come to pass; he shall have whatsoever he saith. Therefore I say unto you, What things soever ye desire, when ye pray, believe that ye receive them, and ye shall have them.

Mark 11:23,24

These are days when we need to have our faith strengthened, when we need to know God. God has designed that the just shall live by faith, no matter how he may be fettered. I know that God's Word is sufficient. One word from Him can change a nation. His Word is from everlasting to everlasting. It is through the entrance of this everlasting Word, this incorruptible seed, that we are born again, and come into this wonderful salvation. Man cannot live by bread alone, but must live by every word that proceedeth out of the mouth of God (Matt. 4:4). This is the food of faith. "...faith cometh by hearing, and hearing by the word of God" (Rom. 10:17).

Everywhere men are trying to discredit the Bible and take from it all the miraculous. One preacher says, "Well, you know, Jesus arranged beforehand to have that colt tied where it was, and for the men to say just what they did." I tell you, God can arrange everything without going near. He can plan for you, and when He plans for you, all is peace. All things are possible if you will believe.

Another preacher said, "It was an easy thing for Jesus to feed the people with five loaves. The loaves were so big in those days that it was a simple matter to cut them into a thousand pieces each." But He forgot that one little boy brought those five loaves all the way in his lunch basket. There is nothing impossible with God. All the impossibility is with us when we measure God by the limitations of our unbelief.

We have a wonderful God, a God whose ways are past finding out, and whose grace and power are limitless. I was in Belfast one day and saw one of the brethren of the assembly. He said to me, "Wigglesworth, I am troubled. I have had a good deal of sorrow during the past five months. I had a woman in my assembly who could always pray the blessing of heaven down on our meetings. She is an old woman, but her presence is always an inspiration. But five months ago she fell and broke her thigh. The doctors put her into a plaster cast, and after five months they broke the cast. But the bones were not properly set and so she fell and broke the thigh again."

He took me to her house, and there was a woman lying in a bed on the right hand side of the room. I said to her, "Well, what about it now?" She said, "They have sent me home incurable. The doctors say that I am so old that my bones won't knit. There is no nutriment in my bones and they could never do anything for me, and they say I shall have to lie in bed for the rest of my life." I said to her, "Can you believe God?" She replied, "Yes, ever since I heard that you had come to Belfast my faith has been quickened. If you will pray, I will believe. I know there is no power on earth that can make the bones of my thigh knit, but I know there is nothing impossible with God." I said, "Do you believe He will meet you now?" She answered, "I do."

It is grand to see people believe God. God knew all about this leg and that it was broken in two places. I said to the woman, "When I pray, something will happen." Her husband was sitting there; he had been in his chair for four years and could not walk a step. He called out, "I don't believe. I won't believe. You will never get me to believe." I said, "All right," and laid my hands on his wife in the name of the Lord Jesus. The moment hands were laid upon her and she cried out, "I'm healed." I said, "I'm not going to assist you to rise. God will do it all." She arose and walked up and down the room, praising God.

The old man was amazed at what had happened to his wife, and he cried out, "Make me walk, make me walk." I said to him, "You old sinner, repent." He cried out, "Lord, You know I believe." I don't think he meant what he said; anyhow the Lord was full of compassion. If He marked our sins, where would any of us be? If we will meet the conditions, God will always meet us, if we believe all things are possible. I laid my hands on him and the power went right through the old man's body, and those legs, for the first time in four years received power to carry his body, and he walked up and down and in and out. He said, "Oh, what great things God has done for us tonight!"

"...What things soever ye desire, when ye pray, believe that ye receive them, and ye shall have them" (Mark 11:24). Desire toward God and you will have desires from God, and He will meet you on the line of those desires when you reach out in simple faith.

A man came to me in one of my meetings who had seen other people healed and wanted to be healed, too. He explained that his arm had been fixed in a certain position for many years and he could not move it. "Got any faith?" I asked. He said that he had a lot of faith. After prayer he was able to swing his arm round and round. But he was not satisfied and complained, "I feel a little bit of trouble just there," pointing to a certain place. I said, "Do you know what the trouble is with you? Imperfect faith." "...What things soever ye desire, when ye pray, believe that ye receive them, and ye shall have them."

Did you believe before you were saved? So many people would be saved, but they want to feel saved first. There was never a man who felt saved before he believed. God's plan is always this, if you will believe, you shall see the glory of God. I believe God wants to bring us all to a definite place of unswerving faith and confidence in Himself.

Jesus here uses the figure of a mountain. Why does He say a mountain? If faith can remove a mountain, it can remove anything. The plan of God is so marvelous, that if you will only believe, all things are possible.

There is one special phrase to which I want to call your attention, "And shall not doubt in his heart." The heart is the mainspring. See that young man and that young woman. They have fallen in love at first sight. In a short while there is a deep affection, and a strong heart love, the one toward the other. What is a heart of love? A heart of faith. Faith and love are kin. In the measure that that young man and that young woman love one another they are true. One may go to the North and the other to the South, but because of their love they will be true to one another.

It is the same when there is a deep love in the heart toward the Lord Jesus Christ. In this new life into which God has brought us, Paul tells us that we have become dead to the law by the body of Christ, that we should be married to another, even to Him who is raised from the dead. God brings us into a place of perfect love and perfect faith. A man who is born of God is brought into an inward affection, a loyalty to the Lord Jesus that shrinks from anything impure. You see the purity of a man and woman when there is a deep natural affection between them; they disdain the very thought of either of them being untrue. I say that in the measure that a man has faith in Jesus he is pure. He that believeth that Jesus is the Christ overcometh the world. It is a faith that worketh by love.

Just as we have heart fellowship with our Lord, our faith cannot be daunted. We cannot doubt in our hearts. There comes, as we go on with God, a wonderful association, an impartation of His very life and nature within. As we read His Word and believe the promises that He has so graciously given to us, we are made partakers of His very essence and life. The Lord is made to us a Bridegroom, and we are His bride. His words to us are spirit and life, transforming us and changing us, expelling that which is natural and bringing in that which is divine.

It is impossible to comprehend the love of God as we think on natural lines. We must have the revelation from the Spirit of God. God giveth liberally. He that asketh, receiveth. God is willing to bestow on us all things that pertain to life and godliness. Oh, it was the love of God that brought Jesus. And it is this same love that helps you and me to believe. In every weakness God will be your strength. You who need His touch, remember that He loves you. Look, wretched, helpless, sick one, away to the God of all grace, whose very essence is love, who delights to give liberally all the inheritance of life and strength and power that you are in need of.

When I was in Switzerland the Lord was graciously working and healing many of the people. I was staying with Brother Reuss of Goldiwil and two policemen were sent to arrest me. The charge was that I was healing the people without a license. Mr. Reuss said to them, "I am sorry that he is not here just now, he is holding a meeting about two miles away, but before you arrest him I would like to show you something."

Brother Reuss took these two policemen down to one of the lower parts of that district, to a house with which they were familiar, for they had often gone to that place to arrest a certain woman who was constantly an inmate of the prison because of continually being engaged in drunken brawls. He took them to this woman and said to them, "This is one of the many cases of blessing that have come through the ministry of the man you have come to arrest. This woman came to our meeting in a drunken condition. Her body was broken, for she was ruptured in two places. While she was drunk, the evangelist laid his hands on her and asked God to heal her and deliver her." The woman joined in, "Yes, and God saved me, and I have not tasted a drop of liquor since." The policemen had a warrant for my arrest, but they said with disgust, "Let the doctors do this kind of thing." They turned and went away and that was the last we heard of them.

We have a Jesus who heals the brokenhearted, who lets the captives go free, who saves the very worst. Dare you, dare you, spurn this glorious Gospel of God for spirit, soul and body? Dare you spurn this grace? I realize that this full Gospel has in great measure been hidden, this Gospel that brings liberty, this Gospel that brings souls out of bondage, this Gospel that brings perfect health to the body, this Gospel of entire salvation. Listen again to this word of Him who left the glory to bring us this great salvation, "...verily I say unto you, That whosoever shall say unto this mountain, Be thou removed...he shall have whatsoever he saith" (Mark 11:23). Whatsoever!

I realize that God can never bless us on the lines of being hardhearted, critical, or unforgiving. This will hinder faith quicker than anything. I remember being at a meeting where there were some people tarrying for the baptism—seeking for cleansing, for the moment a person is cleansed the Spirit will fall. There was one man with eyes red who was weeping bitterly. He said to me, "I shall have to leave. It is no good my staying without I change things. I have written a letter to my brother-in-law, and filled it with hard words, and this thing must first be straightened out." He went home and told his wife, "I'm going to write a letter to your brother and ask him to forgive me for writing to him the way I did." "You fool!" she said. "Never mind," he replied, "this thing is between God and me, and it has got to be cleared away." He wrote the letter and came again, and straightway God filled him with the Spirit.

I believe there are a great many people who would be healed, but they are harboring things in their hearts that are as a blight. Let these things go. Forgive, and the Lord will forgive you. There are many good people, people who mean well, but they have no power to do anything for God. There is just some little thing that came in their hearts years ago, and their faith has been paralyzed ever since. Bring everything to the light. God will sweep it all away if you will let Him. Let the precious blood of Christ cleanse from all sin. If you will but believe, God will meet you and bring into your lives the sunshine of His love.

Published in *The Pentecostal Evangel*

WHAT GOD GIVES,
NO ONE CAN TAKE AWAY
1925

...to another the word of knowledge by the same Spirit; ...to another faith by the same Spirit....

1 Corinthians 12:8,9

We have not passed this way hitherto. I believe that satan has many devices and that they are worse today than ever before; but I also believe that there is to be a full manifestation on the earth of the power and glory of God to defeat every device of satan.

In Ephesians 4, verses 3-6, we are told to endeavor to keep the unity of the Spirit in the bond of peace, for there is one body, and one Spirit, one Lord, one faith, one baptism, and one God and Father of all. The baptism of the Spirit is to make us all one. Paul tells us that "...by one Spirit we are all baptized into one body...and have been all made to drink into one Spirit" (1 Cor. 12:13). It is God's thought that we speak the same thing. If we all have the full revelation of the Spirit of God we shall all see the same thing. Paul asked these Corinthians, "Is Christ divided?" When the Holy Ghost has full control, Christ is never divided, His body is not divided, there is no division. Schism and division are the products of the carnal mind.

How important it is that we shall have the manifestation of "the word of knowledge" in our midst. It is the same Spirit who brings forth the word of wisdom that brings forth the word of knowledge. The revelation of the mysteries of God comes by the Spirit, and we must have a supernatural word of knowledge in order to convey to others the things which the Spirit of God has revealed. The Spirit of God reveals Christ in all His wonderful fullness, and He shows Him to us from the beginning to the end of the Scriptures. It is the Scriptures that make us wise unto salvation, that open to us the depths of the kingdom of heaven which reveal all the divine mind to us.

There are thousands of people who read and study the Word of God. But it is not quickened to them. The Bible is a dead letter except by the Spirit. The words that Christ spoke were not just dead words, but they were spirit and life. And so it is the thought of God that a living word, a word of truth, the Word of God, a supernatural word of knowledge, shall come forth from us through the power of the Spirit of God. It is the Holy Ghost who will bring forth utterances from our lips and a divine revelation of all the mind of God.

The child of God ought to thirst for the Word. He should know nothing else but the Word, and should know nothing among men save Jesus. "...Man shall not live by bread alone, but by every word that proceedeth out of the mouth of God" (Matt. 4:4). It is as we feed on the Word and

MEDITATE ON THE MESSAGE

it contains, that the Spirit of God can vitalize that which we have received, and bring forth through us the word of knowledge that will be as full of power and life as when He, the Spirit of God, moved upon holy men of old and gave them these inspired Scriptures. They were all inbreathed of God as they came forth at the beginning, and through the same Spirit they should come forth from us vitalized, living, powerful, and sharper than any two-edged sword.

With the gifts of the Spirit should come the fruit of the Spirit. With wisdom we should have love, with knowledge we should have joy, and with the third gift, faith, we should have the fruit of peace. Faith is always accompanied by peace. Faith always rests. Faith laughs at impossibilities. Salvation is by faith, through grace, and it is the gift of God. We are kept by the power of God through faith. God gives faith and nothing can take it away. By faith we have power to enter into the wonderful things of God. There are three positions of faith: saving faith, which is the gift of God; the faith of the Lord Jesus; and the gift of faith. You will remember the word of the Lord Jesus Christ given to Paul, to which he refers in Acts 26, where the Lord commissioned him to go to the Gentiles, "To open their eyes, and to turn them from darkness to light, and from the power of Satan unto God, that they may receive forgiveness of sins, and inheritance among them which are sanctified by faith that is in me" (Acts 26:18).

Oh, this wonderful faith of the Lord Jesus. Your faith comes to an end. How many times I have been to the place where I have had to tell the Lord, "I have used all the faith I have," and then He has placed His own faith within me.

One of our workers said to me at Christmas time, "Wigglesworth, I never was so near the end of my purse in my life." I replied, "Thank God, you are just at the opening of God's treasures." It is when we are at the end of our own that we can enter into the riches of God's resources. It is when we possess nothing that we can possess all things.

The Lord will always meet you when you are on the line of living. I was

IN IRELAND

at one time, and went to a house and said to the lady who came to the door, "Is Brother Wallace here?" She replied, "Oh, he has gone to Bangor, but God has sent you here for me. I need you. Come in." She told me her husband was a deacon of the Presbyterian church. She had herself received the baptism while she was a member of the Presbyterian church, but they did not accept it as from God. The people of the church said to her husband, "This thing cannot go on. We don't want you to be deacon any longer, and your wife is not wanted in the church." The man was very enraged and he became incensed against his wife. It seemed as though an evil spirit possessed him, and the home that had once been peaceful became very terrible. At last he left home and left no money behind him, and the woman asked me what should she do.

We went to prayer, and before we had prayed five minutes the woman was mightily filled with the Holy Ghost. I said to her, "Sit down and let me talk to you. Are you often in the Spirit like this?" She said, "Yes, and what could I do without the Holy Ghost now?" I said to her, "The situation is yours. The Word of God says that you have power to sanctify your husband. Dare to believe the Word of God. Now the first thing we must do is to pray that your husband comes back tonight." She said, "I know he won't." I said, "If we agree together, it is done." She said, "I will agree." I said to her, "When he comes home show him all possible love, lavish everything upon him. If he won't hear what you have to say, let him go to bed. The situation is yours. Get down before God and claim him for the Lord. Get into the glory just as you have got in today, and as the Spirit of God prays through you, you will find that God will grant all the desires of your heart."

A month later I saw this sister at a convention. She told how her husband came home that night and that he went to bed, but she prayed right through to victory and then laid hands upon him. He cried out for mercy. The Lord saved him and baptized him in the Holy Spirit. The power of God is beyond all our conception. The trouble is that we do not have the power of God in a full manifestation because of our finite thoughts, but as we go on and let God have His way, there is no limit to what our limitless God will do in response to a limitless faith. But you will never get anywhere except you are in constant pursuit of all the power of God.

One day when I came home from our open-air meeting at 11 o'clock I found that my wife was out. I asked, "Where is she?" I was told that she was down at Mitchell's. I had seen Mitchell that day and knew that he was at the point of death. I knew that it was impossible for him to survive the day unless the Lord undertook.

There are many who let down in sickness and do not take hold of the life of the Lord Jesus Christ that is provided for them. I was taken to see

A WOMAN WHO WAS DYING

and said to her, "How are things with you?" She answered, "I have faith, I believe." I said, "You know that you have not faith, you know that you are dying. It is not faith that you have, it is language." There is a difference between language and faith. I saw that she was in the hands of the devil. There was no possibility of life until he was removed from the premises. I hate the devil, and I laid hold of the woman and shouted,

"Come out, you devil of death. I command you to come out in the name of Jesus." In one minute she stood on her feet in victory.

But to return to the case of Brother Mitchell, I hurried down to the house, and as I got near I heard terrible screams. I knew that something had happened. I passed Mrs. Mitchell on the staircase and asked, "What is up?" She replied, "He is gone! He is gone!" I just passed her and went into the room, and immediately I saw that Mitchell had gone. I could not understand it, but I began to pray. My wife was always afraid that I would go too far, and she laid hold of me and said, "Don't, Dad! Don't you see that he is dead?" I continued to pray and my wife continued to cry out to me, "Don't Dad. Don't you see that he is dead?" But I continued praying. I got as far as I could with my own faith, and then God laid hold of me. Oh, it was such a laying hold that I could believe for anything. The faith of the Lord Jesus laid hold of me, and a solid peace came into my heart. I shouted, "He lives! He lives! He lives!" And he is living today.

There is a difference between our faith and the faith of the Lord Jesus. The faith of the Lord Jesus is needed. We must change faith from time to time. Your faith may get to a place where it wavers. The faith of Christ never wavers. When you have that faith the thing is finished. When you have that faith you will never look at things as they are, you will see the things of nature give way to the things of the Spirit, you will see the temporal swallowed up in the eternal.

I was at a camp meeting in Casaderon, California about eight years ago, and a remarkable thing happened. A man came there who was stone deaf. I prayed for him and I knew that God had healed him. Then came the test. He would always move his chair up to the platform, and every time I got up to speak he would get up as close as he could and strain his ears to catch what I had to say. The devil said, "It isn't done." I declared, "It is done." This went on for three weeks and then the manifestation came and he could hear distinctly 60 yards away. When his ears were opened he thought it was so great that he had to stop the meeting and tell everybody about it. I met him in Oakland recently and he was hearing perfectly. As we remain steadfast and unmoveable on the ground of faith, we shall see what we believe for in perfect manifestation.

People say to me, "Have you not the gift of faith?" I say that it is an important gift, but what is still more important is for us every moment to be making an advancement in God. Looking at the Word of God today I find that its realities are greater to me today than they were yesterday. It is the most sublime, joyful truth that God brings an enlargement. Always an enlargement. There is nothing dead, dry, or barren in this life of the Spirit; God is always moving us on to something higher, and as we move on in the Spirit of faith, it will always rise to the occasion as different circumstances arise.

This is how the gift of faith is manifested. You see an object and you know that your own faith is nothing in the case. The other day I was in San Francisco. I sat in a car and saw a boy in great agonies on the street. I said, "Let me get out." I rushed to where the boy was. He was in agony through cramp of the stomach. I put my hand on his stomach in the name of Jesus. The boy jumped, and stared at me with astonishment. He found himself instantly free. The gift of faith dared in the face of everything. It is as we are in the Spirit that the Spirit of God will operate this gift anywhere and at any time.

When the Spirit of God is operating this gift within a man, He causes him to know what God is going to do. When the man with the withered hand was in the synagogue, Jesus got all the people to look to see what would happen. The gift of faith always knows the results. He said to the man, "Stretch forth thine hand." His word had creative force. He was not living on the line of speculation. He spoke and something happened. He spoke at the beginning and the world came into being. He speaks today and these things have to come to pass. He is the Son of God and came to bring us into sonship. He was the firstfruit of the resurrection, and He calls us to be firstfruits, to be the same kind of fruit like to Himself.

There is an important point here. You cannot have the gifts by mere human desire. The Spirit of God distributes them severally as He wills. God cannot trust some with the gift, but some who have a lowly, broken, contrite heart He can trust. One day I was in a meeting where there were a lot of doctors and eminent men, and many ministers. It was at a convention, and the power of God fell on the meeting.

ONE HUMBLE LITTLE GIRL

who waited tables opened her being to the Lord and was immediately filled with the Holy Ghost and began to speak in tongues. All these big men stretched their necks and looked up to see what was happening and were saying, "Who is it?" Then they learned it was "the servant!" Nobody received but "the servant!" These things are hidden and kept back from the wise and prudent, but the little children, the lowly ones, are the ones who receive. We cannot have faith if we have honor one of another. A man who is going on with God won't accept honor from his fellow beings. God honors the man of a broken, contrite spirit. How shall I get there?

So many people want to do great things, and to be seen doing them, but the one who God will use is the one who is willing to be bidden. My Lord Jesus never said He could do things, but He did them. When that funeral procession was coming up from Nain with the widow's son carried upon the bier, He made them lay it down. He spoke the word, "Arise!" and gave the son back to the widow. He had compassion for her. And you and I will never do anything except on the line of compassion. We will never be able to remove the cancer until we are immersed so deeply into the power of the Holy Ghost that the compassion of Christ is moving through us.

I find that, in all my Lord did, He said that He did not do it, but that another in Him did the work. What a holy submission! He was just an instrument for the glory of God. Have we reached a place where we dare to be trusted with the gift? I see in 1 Corinthians 13 that if I have faith to remove mountains and have not charity, all is a failure. When my love is so deepened in God that I only move for the glory of God, then the gifts can be made manifest. God wants to be manifested, and to manifest His glory to humble spirits.

A faint heart can never have a gift. There are two things essential: first, love; and second, determination—a boldness of faith that will cause God to fulfill His Word. When I was baptized I had a wonderful time and had utterances in the Spirit, but for some time afterward I did not again speak in tongues. But one day as I was helping another, the Lord again gave me utterances in the Spirit. I was one day going down the road and speaking in tongues a long while. There were some gardeners doing their work, and they stuck their heads out to see what was going on. I said, "Lord, You have something new for me. You said that when a man speaks in tongues, he should ask for the interpretation. I ask for the interpretation, and I'll stay right here till I get it." And from that hour the Lord gave me interpretation.

At one time I was in Lincolnshire in England and came in touch with the old

Rector of the Church.

He became very interested and asked me into his library. I never heard anything sweeter than the prayer the old man uttered as he got down to pray. He began to pray, "Lord, make me holy. Lord, sanctify me." I called out, "Wake up! Wake up now! Get up and sit in your chair." He sat up and looked at me. I said to him, "I thought you were holy." He answered, "Yes." "Then what makes you ask God to do what He has done for you?" He began to laugh and then to speak in tongues. Let us move into the realm of faith, and live in the realm of faith, and let God have His way.

Published in *Confidence*

SEEING WITH GOD'S EYES

June 1924

I am pleased to be with you this morning. It is a great joy to be with the saints of God, especially those who have come into "Like Precious Faith" to believe that God is Almighty. Beloved, we may be in a very low ebb of the tide but it is good to be in a place where the tide can rise. I pray that the Holy Ghost shall so have His right of way that there will not be one person in the test who shall not be moved upon by the Spirit of God. Everything depends upon our being filled with the Holy Ghost. And there is nothing you can come short of if the Holy Ghost is the prime mover in your thoughts and life, for He has a plan greater than ours and if He can only get us in readiness for His plan to be worked out, it will be wonderful.

Read Hebrews 11:1-10. This is a very remarkable Word to us, "Faith." Everything depends upon our believing God. If we are saved, it is only because God's Word says so. We cannot rest upon our feelings. We cannot do anything without a living faith. It is surely God Himself who comes to us in the person of His beloved Son and so strengthens us that we realize that our body is surrounded by the power of God, lifting us into the almightiness of His power. All things are possible to us in God. The purpose of God for us is that we might be in the earth for a manifestation of His glory, that every time satanic power is confronted, God might be able to say of us as He did of Job, "What do you think about him?" God wants us so manifested in His divine plan in the earth that satan shall have to hear God. The joy of the Lord can be so manifested in us in this meeting that we shall be so filled with God that we shall be able to rebuke the power of the devil.

God has shown me in the night watches that everything that is not of faith is sin. I have seen this in the Word so many times. God wants so to bring us in harmony with His will that we will see that if we do not come right up to the Word of God, to believe it all, there is something in us that is not purely sanctified to accept the fullness of His Word. Many people are putting their human wisdom right in the place of God and God is not able to give the best because the human is so confronting God. God is not able to get the best through us until the human is dissolved.

"...faith is the substance of things hoped for..." (Heb. 11:1). I want to speak about "substance," it is a remarkable word. Many people come to me and say, "I want things tangible. I want something to appeal to my human reasoning." Brother, everything that you cannot see is eternal. Everything you can see is natural and fadeth away. Everything you see in this tent will fade away and will be consumed but that which you cannot see, which is more real than you, is the substance of all things, which is God in the human soul, mightier than you by a million times. Beloved, we have to go out and be faced with all evil powers. Even your own heart, if it is not entirely immersed in the Spirit, will deceive you. So I am praying that there shall not be a vestige of your human nature that shall not be clothed upon with the power of the Spirit. I pray that the Spirit of the living God may be so imparted to your heart that nothing shall in any way be able to move you after this meeting. "...faith is the substance of things hoped for, the evidence of things not seen" (Heb. 11:1).

God has mightily blessed to me First Peter 1:23:

Being born again, not of corruptible seed, but of incorruptible, by the word of God, which liveth and abideth for ever.

We read, "In the beginning was the Word, and the Word was with God, and the Word was God" (John 1:1). Then we read that "...the Word was made flesh, and dwelt among us, (and we beheld his glory, the glory as of the only begotten of the Father,) full of grace and truth (John 1:14).

And He is in the midst of us manifested. His disciples went out and manifested that they had seen and handled Him, the Word of life.

If you turn to Second Peter 1:4, you will find that we have received His divine nature which is infinite power, infinite knowledge, infinite pleasure, infinite revelation. But people are missing it because we have failed to apply it. But God is making up a people who will have to be "first-fruits." By simple faith you entered in and claimed your rights and became Christians, being born again because you believed. But there is something different in knowing God, in having fellowship with Him; there are heights and depths in this wonderful blessing in the knowledge of Him. Human weakness, helplessness, impossibility. Everybody can see Jacob, but do not forget, beloved, that God changed Jacob into Israel. The Holy Ghost wants everybody to see the unveiling of Jesus. The unveiling of Jesus is to take away yourself and to place Himself in us; to take away all your human weakness and put within you that wonderful Word of eternal power, of eternal life, which makes you believe that all things are possible.

A man traveled with me from Montreal to Vancouver and then on ship to New Zealand. He was a dealer of race horses. It seemed he could not leave me. He was frivolous and talked about races, but he could not keep his end up. I did not struggle to keep up my end because mine is a living power. No person who has Jesus as the inward power of his body needs to be trembling when satan comes around. All he has to do is to stand still and see the salvation of the Lord.

This man entered into a good deal of frivolity and talk of this world. Touching a certain island of the Fiji group, we all went out and God gave me wonderful liberty in preaching. The man came back afterward; he did not go to his racing and card-playing chums. He came stealing back to the ship and with tears in his eyes, he said, "I am dying. I have been bitten by a reptile." His skin had turned to a dark green and his leg was swollen. "Can you help me?" he asked. If we only knew the power of God! If we are in a place of substance, of reality, of ideal purpose, it is not human; we are dealing with almightiness. I have a present God, I have a living faith, and the living faith is the Word and the Word is life, and the Word is equipment, and the Lord is just the same yesterday, and today, and forever (Heb. 13:8). Placing my hand upon the serpent bite, I said, "In the name of Jesus, come out!" He looked at me and the tears came. The swelling went down before his eyes and he was perfect in a moment.

Yes, "Faith is the substance of things hoped for, the evidence of things not seen." Faith is that which came into me when I believed. I was born of the incorruptible Word by the living virtue, life and personality of God. I was instantly changed from nature to grace. I became a servant of God, and I became an enemy of unrighteousness.

The Holy Ghost would have us clearly understand that we are a million times bigger than we know. Every Christian in this place has no conception of what you are. My heart is so big that I want to look in your faces and tell you if you only knew what you had, your body would scarcely be able to contain you. Oh, that God shall so bring us into divine attractiveness by His almightiness that the whole of our bodies shall wake up to resurrection force, to the divine, inward flow of eternal power coursing through the human frame.

Let us read Ephesians 4:7,8,11-13:

> But unto every one of us is given grace according to the measure of the gift of Christ. Wherefore he saith, When he ascended up on high, he led captivity captive, and gave gifts unto men...And he gave some, apostles; and some, prophets; and some, evangelists; and some, pastors and teachers; For the perfecting of the saints, for the work of the ministry, for the edifying of the body of Christ: Till we all come in the unity of the faith, and of the knowledge of the Son of God, unto a perfect man, unto the measure of the stature of the fulness of Christ.

God took you into His pavilion and began to clothe upon you and give you the gifts of the Spirit that in that ministry by the power of God you should bring all the Church into the perfect possession of the fullness of Christ. Oh, the wonder of it! Oh, the adaptability of His equipment!

TONGUES AND INTERPRETATION: "God has designed it. In the pavilion of His splendor, with the majesty of His glory He comes, and touching human weakness, beautifies it in the Spirit of holiness till the effectiveness of this wonderful sonship is made manifest in us, till we all become the edification of the fullness of Christ."

I believe God wants something to be in you this morning that could never be unless you cease to be for yourself. God wants that you should be for God, to be for everybody. But, oh, to have the touch of God! Beloved, the Holy Ghost is the Comforter. The Holy Ghost came not to speak of Himself, but He came to unveil Him who said, "Take my yoke upon you, and learn of me; for I am meek and lowly in heart: and ye shall find rest unto your souls" (Matt. 11:29). The Holy Ghost came to thrill thee with resurrection power and that thou shouldest be anointed with fresh oil running over in the splendor of His almightiness. Then right through thee shall come forth a river of divine unction that shall sustain thee in the bitterest place, and quicken the deadest formality and say to the weak, "Be strong" and to them that have no might, "The Lord of hosts is here to comfort thee." God would have us to be like the rising of the sun, filled with the rays of heaven, all the time beaming forth the gladness of the Spirit of the Almighty. Possibility is the greatest thing of your life.

I came in the tent yesterday afternoon. No one but myself could understand my feelings. Was it emotion? No, it was an inward inspiration to find hearts that God had touched and [that had] met me with such love it was almost more than I could bear. I have to thank God for it and take courage that He has been with me in the past, and He will be with me in the future. Brother and sister, I am satisfied that love is the essential. Love is of God; nay, love is God. Love is the Trinity working in the human to break it up that it may be displaced with God's fullness.

When I was ministering to the sick, there came a man amongst the crowd. If you had seen him, your heart would have ached for him. He was shriveled, weakened, his cheek bones sticking out; eyes sunk, neck all shriveled—just a form. His coat hung on him as you would put it on some stick. He whispered, for he could only speak with a breath of voice, "Can you help me?" I asked, "What is it?" He said that he had had a cancer on his stomach and on the operation table they had taken away the cancer but in the operation they moved the "swallow," so the man could not swallow. He said, "I have tried to take the juice of a cherry today but it would not go down." Then he pulled out a tube about nine inches long, which had a cup at the top. He whispered, "I have a hole in my stomach. As I pour liquid in, my stomach receives that. I have been living three months in that way."

You could call it a shadow of life he was living. Could I help him? Look! This Book can help anybody. This Book is the essence of life. God moves as you believe. This Book is the Word of God. Could I help him? I said, "On the authority of this Word, this night you shall have a big supper." But he said he could not eat. "Do as I tell you," I answered.

"How could it be?" "It is time," I said, "to go and eat a good supper." He went home and told his wife. She could not understand it. She said, "You cannot eat. You cannot swallow." But he whispered, "The man said I had to do it." He got hungry and more hungry and ventured. "I will try it." His wife got it ready. He got a mouth full and it went down just as easy as possible and he went on taking food until he was filled up. Then he and his wife had one of the biggest times of their lives. The next morning he was so full of joy because he had eaten again. He looked down in curiosity to see the hole and found that God had closed it up!

But you ask, "Can He do it for me?" "Yes, if you believe it." Brother, faith is the victory. Here I am, so thankful this morning. Thirty years ago this body you see was sick and helpless and dying. God, in an instant, healed me. I am now 65 years within a day or two and so free and healthy; oh, it is wonderful! There are people in this place who ought to be healed in a moment. People who ought to receive the Holy Ghost in a moment. The power of possibility is in the reach of every man. The Holy Ghost is full of the rising tide. Every one of us can be filled to overflowing. God is here with His divine purpose to change our weakness into mighty strength and faith. The Word of God! Oh, brother, sister, have you got it? It is marrow to your bones. It is unction. It is resurrection from every weakness, it is life from the dead.

If there is anything I want to shake you loose from, it is having a word of faith without the power of it. What are we here for? Surely we are not to hear only, we are to obey. Obedience is better than sacrifice. God the Holy Ghost would give us such a revelation of Christ that we would go away as men who had seen the King. We would go away with our faces lit up with the brilliancy of heaven.

How many in this place are willing to believe? The people who would like God to know they are sincere and they will do whatever His Spirit tells them, rise up and walk to the front and cry to God until you have all you want. Let God have His way. Touch God this morning. Faith is the victory.

Message at Pentecostal Camp Meeting
Berkeley, California

THE BREATH OF GOD
November 1925

Beloved, I believe that God would be pleased for me to read to you from the fifth chapter of St. Mark's gospel, from verse 21 to the end of the chapter. This is a wonderful passage; in fact, all of God's Word is wonderful. It is the Word of life, and it is the impartation of the life of the Savior. Jesus came to give eternal life and He also came to make our bodies whole. I believe that God, the Holy Ghost, wants to reveal the fullness of redemption through the power of Christ's atonement on Calvary until every soul shall get a new sight of Jesus, the Lamb of God. He is lovely. He is altogether lovely. Oh, He is so beautiful! You talk about being decked with the rarest garments, but oh, brother, He could weep with those who weep. He could have compassion on all. There were none that missed His eye.

When He was at the pool, He knew the impotent man and understood his case altogether. Yes, brother, and when He was at Nain, the compassion of the Master was so manifested that it was victorious over death. Do you know that love and compassion are stronger than death? If we touch God, the Holy Spirit, He is the ideal principle of divine life for weaknesses; He is health; He is joy.

God would have us know that He is waiting to impart life. Oh, if thou wouldest believe! Oh, you need not wait another moment. Just now as I preach, receive the impartation of the life by the power of the Word. Do you now know that the Holy Ghost is the breath of heaven, the breath of God, the divine impartation of power that moves in the human and which raises from the dead and quickeneth all things. One of the things that happened on the day of Pentecost in the manifestation of the Spirit was a mighty, rushing wind. The Third Person was manifested in wind, power, mighty, revelation, glory and emancipation. Glory to God! This is why I am on this platform—because of this holy, divine Person who is breath, life, revelation. His power moved me, transformed me, sent me, revised the whole of my position. This wind was the life of God coming and filling the whole place where they were sitting. And when I say to you, "Breathe in," I do not mean merely breathe; I mean breathe in God's life, God's power, the personality of God. Hallelujah!

In the Scripture which we read, we see a man and woman in great trouble. They have a little daughter lying at the point of death. Everything has failed, but they know if they find Jesus, she shall be made whole. Is it possible to seek for Jesus and not find Him? Never! There is not one person in this place who has truly sought for Jesus and has not found Him. As you seek, you will find; as you knock, the door will swing open; as you ask, you will receive. Yes, if you can find Jesus, your little daughter will live. As the Father goes along the road, there is great commotion. He sees the dust rising a long time before he reaches the great company of people who surround Jesus. Hearken to the children's voices and the people shouting. All are delighted because Jesus is in the company. Oh, this camp meeting will rise to a tremendous pitch as we look for Jesus.

Yes, the Father met Him; glory to God! "And besought him greatly, saying, My little daughter lieth at the point of death: I pray thee, come and lay thy hands on her, that she may be healed; and she shall live. And Jesus went with him..." (Mark 5:23,24). I want you to know that this same Jesus is in the midst of His people today. He is right here with His ministry of power and blessing.

But as Jesus went with the man, something happened. "...a certain woman, which had an issue of blood twelve years...came in the press behind, and touched his garment" (Mark 5: 25,27). This poor woman was in an awful state. She had spent all her money on physicians and was "...nothing bettered, but rather grew worse." This poor woman said, "...If

I may touch but His clothes...I shall be whole." No doubt she thought of her weakness, but faith is never weak. She may have been very weary, but faith is never weary. The opportunity had come for her to touch Him and "...straightway the fountain of her blood was dried up; and she felt in her body that she was healed of that plague" (Mark 5:29).

The opportunity comes to you now to be healed. Will you believe? Will you touch Him? There is something in a living faith that is different from anything else. I have seen marvelous things accomplished just because people said, "Lord, I believe." Jesus knew that virtue had gone out of Him and He said, "Who touched me?" The woman was fearful and trembling, but she fell down before the Lord and told Him all the truth. "And he said unto her, Daughter, thy faith hath made thee whole; go in peace, and be whole of thy plague" (Mark 5:34).

"While he yet spake, there came from the ruler of the synagogue's house certain which said, Thy daughter is dead: why troublest thou the Master any further?" (Mark 5:35). But Jesus encouraged the ruler of the synagogue and said, "...Be not afraid, only believe" (Mark 5:36). Ah, what things God does for us when we only believe. He is so rich to all who call upon Him. What possibilities there are in this meeting if we would only believe in the divine presence, for God is here. The power of the Spirit is here. How many of you dare rise and claim your healing? Who will dare rise and claim your rights of perfect health? All things are possible to him who believeth. Jesus is the living substance of faith. You can be perfectly adjusted by the blood of Jesus. We must believe in the revelation of the Spirit's power and see our blessed position in the risen Christ.

Only believe! Only believe! All things are possible, Only believe! "For as the lightning cometh out of the east, and shineth even unto the west; so shall also the coming of the Son of man be" (Matt. 24:27).

Portion of message delivered at Camp Meeting
Berkeley, California

PERPETUAL
DIVINE MOTION
December 1925

Praise the Lord. Praise the Lord. Only believe. All things are possible. Only believe. Absolute dependency. God only. His grand will. Only believe.

What Abraham our father as pertaining to the flesh hath found. What hath Abraham found as pertaining to the flesh? (Rom. 4:1) Something wonderful through God the Holy Ghost. Also seeing that all flesh is as grass, and that in me, that is in my flesh dwelleth no good thing, what hath Abraham our father found pertaining to the flesh? Only this, for the believer God has some One who can live in the flesh, hold the flesh by the power of God above sin and judgment. Jesus Christ, the center of the life where the body, the flesh, has come to the place of being inhabited by God, where God, dwelling in these earthly temples, can live and reign supreme.

He hath quickened that which was dead, bringing life and immortality to light through the Gospel, and the Son of God is manifested there.

God has for us wonderful things. Many days in the past have been wonderful, but no day is like the present. The Holy Ghost lifting us into

His presence, the power flowing, our whole being flaming with the glory of God. Here is God's divine plan for humanity when the Holy Ghost has come. Today we are nearer the goal, the vision is clearer, the Holy Ghost is bringing us into the treasure of the Most High. What hath our father Abraham pertaining to the flesh? I depend upon the Holy Ghost to bring us into revelation. There is no room for weakness if we see this mighty incoming life through the Spirit.

OBEY GOD

What hath our father Abraham found pertaining to the flesh? He found that as he heard the voice of God and obeyed it, it not only judged him but wonderful things were manifested. One day away there God said to Abraham, Come out. God has wonderful things to say to you if you come to the hearing of faith, not the natural order, taste, desire, affection. Oh yes, if God gets your ear you will come out.

One day God said to me, Come out. I had not been in long. I was in the Wesleyan Church. Was there anything wrong? No. Only God said, Come out. He had something further. The Salvation Army was in full swing. I was very anxious to get the best. Revival was at full, but they turned to other things. So God said, Come out. We need to have the hearing of faith, always soaring higher, understanding the leading of the Spirit. Oh, the breath of God. Then I went to the Brethren, they had the Word, but so much of the letter with it, and splitting of hairs. God said, Come out. Oh, they said, he has gone again, there is no satisfying him. Then came the baptism of the Holy Ghost, with signs following according to Acts 2. God alone speaking. Faith bringing us to a place of revelation to cover us and God coming in and manifesting His power.

What had our father Abraham found pertaining to the flesh? Two things: (1) A righteousness by law; and, (2) a righteousness by faith. Believing what God says, and daring on the authority of God's Word to act. God will meet us there, within that blessed place, making for us opportunities of blessing. Love, truth, revelation, manifestation. God and you in activity, bringing divine ability and activity into action.

> Oh it's all right now, it's all right now,
> For Jesus is my Savior,
> So it's all right now.

The way into the treasure house of the Most High is the authority of the living Word. The kingdom of heaven is open to all believers.

He has called us, bringing us into divine association with heaven, if we will dare to believe, for all things are possible to him who believeth.

When we believe, we shall find, like Abraham who believed God, tremendous ability, changing weakness into strength, character, power, association within, making all things new. A life yielded, absorbed by divine authority. Standing on the principles of God.

In Wellington, New Zealand, there was a crowd of needy people come for help, among them a heavy built woman. God revealed to me the presence of the enemy within the body. She cried out, "You are killing me," and fell down in the aisle. I said, "Lift her up. God is not done yet." The onlookers in judgment didn't know, but three yards off she was loosed from a cancer. It is wise to believe God. God has a place for the man or woman who dares to believe. The man God has His hand on is not subject to the opinions of others. This our father Abraham found pertaining to the flesh. May God increase the number who dare to believe under all circumstances. To dare to believe God on the authority of the Word.

I came across a peculiar case. A man bent double, he was in agony, cancer on the bladder, he cried and cried. I said, "Do you believe God?" He said, "No, I have nothing in common with God." I tried to bring him to the place of believing, but his mental capacity was affected. I said, "I see you don't understand, it may be God wants me to help you." I said the Name of Jesus. What is it? It is the One who met us at Calvary, come with new life divine.

Before all the message, God means us to be an extraordinary people with this wonderful life of faith in the body. Abraham found, when he believed God, that he was bound to Almighty power, equipped for service, by faith.

Laying my hands on the sick man in the Name, I didn't have to say, "Are you whole?" He knew he was whole. He couldn't tell what he had got. This man had been interested in yachts, he was a member of a yacht club. His friends went as usual to see him and began talking about yachts. He said, "Yachts! Yachts! Talk to me about Jesus!" Oh yes, there is something in the Name. Our father Abraham pertaining to the flesh found it. The Word of God the link, the key, the personality of divine equipment. There is something mighty in believing God. Have you found it? A faith that believes God apprehends what God said. What did God say? God said that because Abraham believed Him He would cover him with His righteousness, holiness, and integrity of faith. God loves to see His children when they believe Him. He covers them. It is a lovely covering, the covering of the Almighty. Blessed is the man to whom God imputeth righteousness. Is it to be?

God has for us a perfect work, a hearing of faith that has within the sound of His voice, hearing Him speak, our speech betraying us. Epistles of the divine character having His life, passion, and compassion. Beloved, there must be this divine fellowship between us and God.

The disciples said: What shall we do to do the works of God? Jesus said: This is the work of God that ye believe on Him Whom He hath sent.

CHRIST DWELLING WITHIN BY FAITH

This is what our father Abraham pertaining to the flesh hath found. A written epistle, known and read of all men. Paul was enamored of it. He followed this divine fire with all that are in the faith with Abraham. When Paul speaks in Ephesians and Colossians we see what he with Abraham had received pertaining to the flesh, Christ in you the hope of glory. It's all embedded there, all we need, filled unto all the fullness of God.

The baptism in the Holy Ghost crowns Jesus King in His royal palace. When the King is crowned what tremendous things we find pertaining to the flesh. Perpetual divine motion. The power of God sweeping through the regions of weakness. What have we got pertaining to the flesh? New life flowing through. All the Word of God is Yea and Amen to faith. Divine actions in the human frame mighty, so full of operation till we see God working. For these young men and women I see such possibilities in coming into line with God, nothing can interfere with the progress of God, the Author of life and Finisher of faith. Never be afraid of your voice when the Spirit is upon you, nor living for yourself but with a ministry of freedom.

First Corinthians 12. No man can call Jesus Lord but in the Holy Ghost. I see the dew of the Spirit, the order of blessing, ability to crown Jesus King, set apart for God.

Then there is the sealing of the Spirit, the great adjusting, giving us the knowledge in the revelation of Jesus as King over all, affections, desires, wishes; all His.

His compassion, His meekness, His dynamic—the power to move the devil away. A big plan—a force of unity, a divine capacity—making things move.

A man and his wife came to me troubled about things taking place in their meeting. I said: You two can be so perfectly joined in unity, as to take victory for every meeting, not a thing could stand against you, a perfect fellowship, which the devil is not able to break, if any two of you agree. Dare on the authority of God's Word to bind every spirit in the meeting.

A faith pertaining to our flesh manifested in human bodies, circumcision for home affairs, financial difficulties, more than conquerors in this operation of faith.

Romans 4:16. It is of faith that it might be of grace that the promise might be sure to all the seed. Nothing is so large, inhabited by this operation of faith that is brought to us through Calvary. Mighty revival, I feel it coming, my whole being moves toward it. I dare to believe in simplicity of faith.

Once in Norway, the halls were packed and the streets thronged to hear God's Word, we want it in London. God has given us a divine plan to operate with Him. The deluge can come, a Pentecostal outpouring for the glory of God.

There is now a way into the kingdom of heaven by faith. No reserve on God's side, only believe, to see the mighty power of God fall, we are here to awake you.

Abraham was tested. God is greater than the testing and opens a door of deliverance. Faith! God never changes. What had Abraham received? Testing. But called, chosen and faithful, faithful to God in the trial; 25 years Abraham waited—he believed against hope, giving glory to

God. Not one thing will fail if you dare believe. All fullness in manifestation arising in faith, all needs of the body met in a moment on the word of faith, give God the glory, stammering tongue, consumption, neurasthenia, need of salvation, all needs met if we dare believe. We are in the place of receiving all our father Abraham did, pertaining to the flesh. Let us put in our claim, letting the deluge come that God wants to send.

Romans 4:20,21. Giving glory to God, becoming strong in faith, being fully persuaded that what He has promised He is able also to perform. That God may be glorified in us and we in Him, having found as Abraham did, the hearing of faith. The righteousness that is ours through faith. Amen.

Published in *Redemption Tidings*

THE ROCK FAITH
November 1926

Only believe. To so hear the Word of God by the Spirit's power. Changed by the grace of God. Changed by the revelation of God. Only believe. Other refuge have I none.

If thou wilt believe. Awake to the fact, knowing the Scriptures, resting unconditionally, absolutely upon the Word of God. God has never failed anyone relying upon His Word. Some human plan or your mind may come between, but rest upon what God's Word says. Only believe. Oh the charm of the truth, making you rich forever, taking away all weariness. Those who put their trust in God are like Mount Zion. They cannot be moved. Rock of Ages cleft for me. Oh, the almightiness of God's plan for us, tremendous. We are only weak and helpless when we forget the visitation of the Lord. From the uttermost to the uttermost. Ask and ye shall receive, seek and ye shall find, knock and it shall be opened unto you.

HIS ROCK—THIS ROCK

When Jesus came into the coasts of Caesarea Phillippi, he asked his disciples, saying, Whom do men say that I the Son of man am? ...And Simon Peter answered and said, Thou art the Christ, the Son of the living God. And Jesus answered and said unto him,

Blessed art thou, Simon Bar-jona: for flesh and blood hath not revealed it unto thee, but my Father which is in heaven. And I say also unto thee, That thou art Peter, and upon this rock I will build my church; and the gates of hell shall not prevail against it. And I will give unto thee the keys of the kingdom of heaven: and whatsoever thou shalt bind on earth shall be bound in heaven: and whatsoever thou shalt loose on earth shall be loosed in heaven.

Matthew 16:13,16-19

Jesus was full of ideals, perfect in those He was dealing with. Jesus came with a perfect purpose that many might hear and live and come into apostolic conditions, divine life. Jesus was a firstfruit to bring to the disciples a knowledge that they were in a divine act to supersede every last power in the world. Holiness is the keynote. Saving grace is a revelation from heaven. Christ within sets up the heavenly standard, the heavenly mind, so that we live, act and think in a new world.

Whom do men say that I, the Son of man, am? Then Peter, with eyes and heart aflame said, "You are the Christ, the Son of the living God." Jesus perceiving in a moment that the revelation had come from heaven said, "Blessed art thou Simon Bar-jona, for flesh and blood hath not revealed it unto thee, but My Father in heaven." God's great plan is that His children should be salt for a world diseased. Ye are the salt of the earth, ye are the light of the world. To be saved is to have the revelation of the glory of Christ, it is our inheritance to have the evidence of the Holy Ghost coming upon us. Sons with power, manifestations of the Son, built upon the faith of the Son of God. Upon this Rock will I build My Church, and the gates of hell shall not prevail against it.

God is visiting the earth with His resplendent glory. His coming is to revive, to heal, to deliver from the power of the pit. The ransom is the Lord, and He comes to save the oppressed, whose eyes, ears, and heart shall see, hear, and feel with a new beauty.

IMPREGNABLE FAITH

In the innermost soul of the Holy Ghost abiding in power, for the King has come to fill and rule the body, and transform the life. A new creature, a perfect preservation and manifestation over all the powers of evil, pure and holy. He is so sweet. He is the most lovely of all. The bruised reed He will not break nor quench the smoking flax. God has designed, by the Holy Ghost, to bring forth character divine. As He is, so are we in this world. God has saved and chosen and equipped that those bound by satan may go free. Jesus is speaking to the disciples on a plan of ministry. "Verily, verily, I say unto you, He that believeth on me, the works that I do shall he do also; and greater works than these shall he do; because I go unto my Father" (John 14:12), laying emphasis on the fact of this truth, faith, and Christ's Rock are one and the same structure, rock! Upon this Rock I will build My Church, and the gates of hell shall not prevail against it. Rock!

Emblematic of a living faith, a divine principle, what God the Holy Ghost has to create and bring forth within us. No devil or evil power should be allowed to remain where we are. Jesus was teaching His disciples that as they believed greater things would be accomplished because He was going. Upon this Rock! Upon this living faith will I build My Church. Whatsoever ye bind or loose on earth shall be bound or loosed in heaven, (Matt. 16:19). Keep in mind this word, satan has tremendous power in the world, and people suffer as they never would if they only knew the truth, which cannot be gainsaid. Upon this Rock will I build My Church. The Kingdom, the new birth come with power, upon this Rock, this living faith. This awful responsibility, that unless I believe and act on this Word, it will not be operative in others.

Ninety percent and more diseases are satanic power. How many here received a touch from Jesus this afternoon, and were loosed from their pains? How was this accomplished? By binding and destroying the evil power in the Name of Jesus. Not only are we given power to loose and bind, but Jesus says the gates of hell shall not prevail against His Church. There must be the fellowship of Christ's sufferings. He has suffered for the people, there must be an entering in, a compassion, we are to be moved in union with needy sufferers. Jesus was moved with compassion. Oh, the compassion of Jesus! We must be moved, the compassion taking us to the place of delivering the people. God knows all about this meeting, and we have power to bind or loose in the Name of Jesus. Who would believe?

Have ye received the Holy Ghost since ye believed? After God has saved you by His power He wants you to be illuminators of the King, new creations. The King is already on the throne, the Holy Ghost has come to reveal the fullness of power of His ministry. To be filled with the Holy Ghost is to be filled with prophetic illumination. The baptism in the Holy Ghost brings divine utterance, the divine bringing out pure prophecy. Then it becomes a condition. God is our foundation, the Word of God is our standing. We are here to glorify God. I know how weak I am. Struggle, are we to struggle? No, no! Believe what God has said. We must be in our place ready for the opportunity. God wants to give us divine life from heaven. The gates of hell shall not prevail against it. The rock of deliverance by the key of faith. You shall open the kingdom of heaven and shut the gates of hell. You shall bind and loose in Jesus' Name.

He cometh with the truth. Know His strength for the broken and the helpless. He revealeth His strength. A great tide of revival spirit, clothed with His Spirit, the Lord shall give thee light. Fall down and worship Him.

Ask what ye will. Whatsoever things ye desire when ye pray, believe! Believe! Ye shall have them!

THE WORD THAT COMES
WITH POWER
July 16, 1927

Be not afraid, only believe.

Mark 5:36

This is one of those marvelous truths of the Scriptures that is written for our help, that we may believe as we see the almightiness of God and also our privilege, not only to enter in by faith, but to become partakers of the blessing He wants to give us. My message is on the lines of faith. Because some do not hear in faith, it profits them nothing. There is a hearing of faith and a hearing that means nothing more than listening to words. I beseech you to see to it that everything done may bring not only blessing to you but strength and character, and that you may be able to see the goodness of God in this meeting.

I want to impress upon you the importance of believing what the Scripture says, and I may have many things to relate about people who dared to believe God until it came to pass. This is a wonderful Word. In fact, all of the Word of God is wonderful. It is an everlasting Word, a Word of power, a Word of health, a Word of substance, a Word of life. It gives life into the very nature, to everyone that lays hold of it, if he believes. I want you to understand that there is a need for the Word of

God. But it is a need, many times, that brings us the blessing. What am I here for? Because God delivered me when no other hand could do it. I stand before you as one who was given up by everybody, when no one could help. I was earnest and zealous for the salvation of souls. If you were in Bradford (England), you would know. We had police protection for nearly 20 years in the best thoroughfare in the city, and in my humble way with my dear wife, who was all on fire for God, we were ministering in the open air. Full of zeal? Yes. But one night, 30 years ago, I was carried home helpless. We knew very little about divine healing, but we prayed through. It is 30 years and more since God healed me. I am 68 years old and fresher, in better health, and more fit for work than I was at that time. It is a most wonderful experience when the life of God becomes the life of man. The divine power that sweeps through the organism, cleaning the blood, makes the man fresh every day. The life of God is resurrection power.

When they brought me home helpless we prayed all night. We did all we knew. At ten o'clock the next morning I said to my wife, "This must be my last roll call." We had five children around us. I tell you it was not an easy thing to face our circumstances. I told my wife to do as she thought best but the poor thing didn't know what to do. She called a physician who examined me, shook his head and said, "It is impossible for anything to be done for your husband; I am absolutely helpless. He has appendicitis and you have waited too long. His system will not stand an operation. A few hours, at best, will finish him."

What the doctor said was true. He left her and said he would come back again but he couldn't give her any hope. When he was nicely out of the house an old lady and a young man who knew how to pray came in. The young man put his knees on the bed and said: "Come out, you devil, in the name of Jesus." It was a good job, we had no time for argument, and instantly I was free. Oh, hallelujah! I was as free as I am now. I never believed that any person ought to be in bed in the daytime and I jumped up and went downstairs. My wife said: "Oh, are you up?" "I'm all right, wife; it is all right now," I said. I had some men working for me and she said none of them had turned up that morning, so I picked up my tools and went to work. Then the doctor came. He walked up the stairs and my wife called, "Doctor, doctor, he is out!" "What?" he said. "Yes," she said, "He is out at work." "Oh," he said, "you will never see him alive again.

They will bring him in a corpse." Am I a corpse? Oh, when God does anything it is done forever! And God wants you to know that He wants to do something in you forever. I have laid my hands on people with appendicitis when the doctors were in the place, and God has healed them.

I will tell you one incident before I pass on. It will stir up your faith. I am not here to be on exhibition. I am here to impart divine truth to you concerning the Word of God that after I leave you can do the same thing. I went to Switzerland and after I had been there for some weeks, a brother said, "Will you not go to meeting tonight?" "No," I said, "I have been at it all this time, you can take charge tonight." "What shall we do?" he asked. "Do?" I said, "Paul the apostle, left people to do the work and passed on to another place—I have been here long enough now, you do the work." So he went to the meeting. When he came back he said, "We have had a wonderful time." "What happened?" He said: "I invited them all out, took off my coat, and rolled up my sleeves, and prayed and they were all healed. I did just like you did." Jesus says, "I give unto you power over all the power of the enemy" (Luke 10:19). They entered into the houses and healed the sick that were therein. The ministry of divine operation in us is wonderful, but who would take upon himself to say, "I can do this or that?" If it is God, it is all right, but if it is yourself, it is all wrong. When you are weak, then you are strong. When you are strong in your own strength, you are weak. You must realize this and live only in the place where the power of God rests upon you, and where the Spirit moves within you. Then God will mightily manifest His power and you will know as Jesus said, "The Spirit of the Lord is upon me."

God brings a remarkable, glorious fact to our minds tonight, the healing of a little helpless girl. The physicians had failed. The mother said to the father: "There is only one hope—if you can see Jesus! As sure as you can meet Jesus our daughter will live." Do you think it is possible for anybody anywhere to go looking for Jesus without seeing Him? Is it possible to think about Jesus without Jesus drawing near? No. This man knew the power there was in the name of Jesus: "...In my name shall they cast out devils..." (Mark 16:17). But we must be sure we know that Name, for in Acts 19 the seven sons of Sceva said to the man possessed with devils, "We adjure you by Jesus whom Paul preached to come out" (Acts 19:13). The evil spirit said, "I know Paul and I know Jesus, but who are you?" (Acts 19:15). Yes, the devil knows every believer—and the seven sons of Sceva nearly lost their lives. The evil powers came upon them and they barely escaped. It is more than repeating the Name; it is the nature of the Name in you; it is more than that; it is the divine personality within the human life which has come to take up His abode in you, and when He becomes all in all then God works through you. It is the life, the power of God. God works through the life.

The Lord is that life, and the ministry of it and the power in the ministry, but the Holy Spirit brings everybody in such a place of divine relationship that He mightily lives in us and enables us to overcome the powers of the enemy. The Lord healed that child as they got a vision of Jesus. The Word of the Lord came not with observation but with divine, mighty power, working in them until by the power of the Spirit, men and women were created anew by this new life divine. We have to see that when this divine Word comes to us by the power of the Holy Ghost, it is according to the will of God that we speak, not with men's wisdom, but with divine minds operated by the Word of God; not channels only, but as oracles of the Spirit.

As the ruler of the synagogue sought Jesus he worshiped Him. How they gathered around Him! How everybody listened to what He had to say! He spoke not as a scribe, but with authority and power, decked with divine glory. A young man was preaching in a marketplace. At the close of the address some atheist came and said, "There have been five Christs. Tell us which one it is that you preach." He answered, **"The Christ that rose from the dead."** There is only One that rose from the dead. There is only one Jesus who lives. And as He lives, we live also. Glory to God! We are risen with Him, are living with Him, and will reign with Him.

This ruler, as he drew near the crowd, went up to Him and said, "Jesus, my daughter lieth at the point of death. Come and lay thy hands upon her, and she will be healed." [And Jesus went with him.] (See Mark 5:23,24.) What a beautiful assurance. But as they were coming along the road, a woman met them who had an issue of blood for 12 years. When she began with this trouble she sought many physicians. She had some money, but the physicians took it all, and left her worse than they found her. Have you any that do the same thing around here? When I was a plumber I had to finish my work before I got the money, and I didn't always get it then. I think that if there was an arrangement whereby no doctor got his fee until he cured the patient, there wouldn't be so many people die. Twelve years of sickness this woman had. She needed someone now who could heal without money, for she was bankrupt and helpless. Jesus comes to people that are withered up, diseased, lame, crippled in all kinds of ways, and when He comes there is liberty to the captive, opening of eyes to the blind, and the opening of ears to the deaf. Many had said to this woman, "If you had only been with us today. We saw the most marvelous things, the crooked made straight, the lame to walk, the blind to see"—and the woman 12 years sick said, "Oh, you make me feel that if I could only see Him I should be healed." It strengthened her faith and it became firm. She had a purpose within her. Faith is a mighty power. Faith will reach at everything. When real faith comes into operation you will not say, "I don't feel much better." Faith says, "I am whole." Faith doesn't say, "It's a lame leg." Faith says, "My leg is all right." Faith never sees a goiter.

A young woman with a goiter came to be prayed for. In a testimony meeting she said, "I do praise the Lord for healing my goiter." She went home and said to her mother, "Oh Mother, when the man prayed for me, God healed my goiter." For 12 months she went about telling everybody how God healed her goiter. Twelve months afterward I was in the same place and people said, "How big that lady's goiter is!" There came a time for testimony. She jumped up and said, "I was here 12 months ago and God healed me of my goiter. Such a marvelous 12 months!" when she went home her folks said, "You should have seen the people today when you testified that God had healed your goiter. They think there is something wrong with you. If you go upstairs and look in the glass you will see the goiter is bigger than ever it was." She went upstairs, but she didn't look in the glass. She got down on her knees and said, "O Lord, let all the people know just as You have let me know, how wonderfully You have healed me." The next morning her neck was as perfect as any neck you ever saw. Faith never looks. Faith praises God—it is done!

This poor, helpless woman who had been growing weaker and weaker for 12 years pushed into the crowded thoroughfare when she knew Jesus was in the midst. She was stirred to the depths, and she pushed through and touched Him. If you will believe God and touch Him, you will be healed at once. Jesus is the Healer!

Now listen! Some people put the touch of the Lord in the place of faith. The Lord would not have that woman believe that the touch had done it. She felt as soon as she touched Him that virtue had gone through her, which is true. When the people were bitten by fiery serpents in the wilderness, God's Word said through Moses, "He that looketh shall be healed." The look made it possible for God to do it. Did the touch heal the woman? No. The touch meant something more—it was a living faith. Jesus said, "...thy faith hath made thee whole..." (Mark 5:34). If God would just move on us to believe, there wouldn't be a sick person who could not receive healing. As soon as this woman in the street, with all the crowd about her, began to testify, the devil came. The devil is always in a testimony meeting. When the sons of God gathered together in the time of Job, he was there.

While this was happening in the street, [a] person came rushing from the house of Jairus and said, "There is no use now, your daughter is dead. This Jesus can do nothing for a dead daughter. Your wife needs you at home." But Jesus said, "Be not afraid, only believe" (Mark 5:36). He speaks the word just in time! Jesus is never behind time. When the tumult is the worst, the pain the most severe, the cancer gripping the body, then the word comes, "Only believe." When everything seems as though it will fail, and is practically hopeless, the Word of God comes to us, "Only believe."

When Jesus came to that house there were a lot of people weeping and wailing. I have taken my last wreath to the cemetery. To be absent from the body is to be present with the Lord, and if you believe that, you will never take another wreath to the cemetery. It is unbelief that mourns. If you have faith that they are with the Lord, you will never take another flower to the grave. They are not there. Hallelujah!

These people were round about, weeping, wailing, and howling. He says, "Why make you this ado? The maid is not dead, but sleepeth" (Mark 5:39). There is a wonderful word that God wants you to hear. Jesus said, "I am the resurrection, and the life..." (John 11:25). The believer may fall asleep, but the believer doesn't die. Oh, that people would understand the deep things of God—it would change the whole situation. It makes you look out with a glorious hope to the day when the Lord shall come. What does it say? "They that sleep will God bring with Him." Jesus knew that. "The maid is not dead, but sleepeth; and they laughed him to scorn" (Mark 5:39,40). To show the insincerity of these wailers, they could turn from wailing to laughing. Jesus took the father and the mother of the maid and, going into the room where she was, took her hand and said, "Daughter, arise." And the child sat up. Praise the Lord! And He said, "Give her something to eat."

Oh, the remarkableness of our Lord Jesus! I want to impress upon you the importance of realizing that He is in the midst. No person need be without the knowledge that they are not only saved, but that God can live in these bodies. You are begotten the moment you believe, unto a lively hope. "He that believeth **hath eternal life.**" You have eternal life the moment you believe. The first life is temporal, natural, material, but in the new birth you exist as long as God—forever—we are begotten by an incorruptible power, by the Word of God. The new birth is unto righteousness, begotten by God the moment that you believe. God always saves through the heart. He that believeth in the heart and confesseth with his mouth shall be saved.

Jesus is here tonight to loose them who are bound. If you are suffering in your body. He will heal you now as we pray. He is saying to every sin-sick soul, to every disease-smitten one. "Be not afraid, Only believe."

Published in *The Pentecostal Evangel*

A POWER GREATER THAN NATURE'S POWER

October 1927

We will read from Hebrews 11. This is one of the greatest subjects there is from Genesis to Revelation. It is impossible to bring to you anything greater than the nature of God. We have now entered not in the covenant but the very nature of God, the divine nature, through faith. God has all thoughts and all knowledge, and we may have glimpses of His divine life. The Word of God is life. Jesus was made flesh and He came in the flesh for this very purpose to move people. Yes, beloved, the Creator was in the midst of creation. He opened blind eyes, unstopped deaf ears, made the lame walk; but He had all knowledge.

It is a new birth and just as we allow natural things to cease; then He comes in, in all His fullness. But you say, can we be in and out. Yes, if He comes in, the old man goes out; we can become out and out. Now I believe this morning's plan is for us all, but we must get into the real spirit of it. Beloved, do not stumble if you cannot move mountains; oh no, there may be some molehills need moving first. "Greater is He that is in you, than he that is in the world" (1 John 4:4). God has no need of a man who is hot today and cold tomorrow; He needs men who are hot today and hotter tomorrow and still hotter the next day—that is the man who is going to touch the glory. The Lord never changes, He is just the same; if you change it does not mean to say God has changed. I am amazed all the while at what God is doing—it is from glory to glory. Now, it is no good unless we have a foundation; but, glory to God, our foundation is the most powerful and unmovable foundation—it is the very Word of God. When we are born again we are born of a substance— the Word of God—no corruption in it, the incorruptible Word of God. I believe when a man is born again he gets knowledge how to sow the Word of God in such a way that will bring another into the same knowledge. Everyone who is born again can sow. Now, when Jesus said God so loved the world, it was an immeasurable sow—it's a fact that is worked in and has to come out; but it is the plan of God, and you are all in it this morning, and I believe that there can be such an enlargement in us that will swallow us up, and if you are not in that place, then you must be a back number. But remember this, we have all more than we are using.

Now I want to dwell a little on this word substance. We must build ourselves up in the most holy faith; do not stop running in the race—it is an awful thing for a person to run and then stop, and someone else get the prize. Paul speaks on this line in 1 Corinthians 9:24.

Know ye not that they which run in a race run all... So run, that ye may obtain.

Also he says in Philippians 3:12:

Not as though I had already attained, either were already perfect: but I follow after, if that I may apprehend that for which also I am apprehended of Christ Jesus.

So he cries out, I press toward the mark. It is a disgrace to God for a person just to keep pace. We must press on; if you are making no headway, you must be a backslider, because you have had such opportunities. Now, substance is the evidence of things not seen.

Right in every born-again person there is that power which is greater than the natural force. God says twice in one chapter "...lay hold on eternal life," (1 Tim. 6:12,19) a thing you cannot see, and yet we have to lay hold of it.

Now, beloved, we must pass more than anything we have passed before. I really mean all I say. I am not speaking from the abundance of my mind, but my heart. The abundance of the mind makes swelled heads, but we want swelled hearts. I want to make you all drunk with new wine. We can have this treasure in earthen vessels. God does not want you to be natural people. He wants you to be people who will cut through anything. Born into God's life, the new birth is life, the life of God. Christ in you, the hope of glory. No person can go on in this way and stand still. Love the Word of God. "In the beginning was the Word, and the Word was with God, and the Word was God" (John 1:1). Jesus was the only begotten of the Father, full of grace and truth. Perhaps you have never known before what God wants you to possess. Now take these words:

> *Through faith we understand that the worlds were framed by the word of God, so that things which are seen were not made of things which do appear.*
>
> *Hebrews 11:3*

My word if you do not all become big today—I do not mean in your own estimation. Now when you first came into the world you were made, but when you were born again you were begotten. Now read John 1:1-3:

> *In the beginning was the Word, and the Word was with God, and the Word was God. The same was in the beginning with God. All things were made by him; and without him was not any thing made that was made.*
>
> *John 1:1-3*

So you see, all things were made by Him. Oh, beloved, He will act if you will let Him have a chance. What do I mean? Well, listen! A man came to me and said, "Can you help me, I cannot sleep, and my nerves are terrible."

Now Jesus put a principle in the Word of God, He said, "Ask anything in My name and I will do it," so I prayed for the man, and said, "Now go home and sleep in the name of Jesus"; he said, "But I can't sleep"; I said "Go home and sleep," and gave him a push. So he went, and according to the Word of God, he went home and slept, and he slept so long his wife went to wake him up, but, thinking he was tired, let him sleep on; but he slept all Saturday, and the poor wife did not know what to do; but the man awoke, and was so changed he got up and went about shouting, "I am a new man, praise the Lord."

What had done it? Why, it was the Word of God, and we have the Word in us, the faith of the Son of God. Now we can all have from God this morning what we believe for. If you want anything, put your hands up. If you are in earnest, walk out to the front. And if you are really desperate, run out. Amen.

Published in *Redemption Tidings*

LIVING FAITH,
DEAD FAITH
January 1930

Praise God! It is a great joy to see you all. There is something that brings us all here. What will it be when we get rid of this body of flesh, and when Jesus is the light of the city of God? Nevertheless, God means for us while here to put on the whole armour of God. He wants us to be covered with the covering of His Spirit, and to grow in grace and the knowledge of God. Oh, what God has laid up for us, and what we may receive through the name of Jesus! Oh, the value of the name, the power of the name; the very name of Jesus brings help from heaven, and the very name of Jesus can bind evil powers and subdue all things unto Himself. Thank God for victory through our Lord Jesus Christ.

For the sake of saving us, He endured the cross, despising the shame. How beautiful it is to say with our whole will, "I will be obedient unto God." Oh, He is lovely, He is beautiful—I never remember coming to Him when He once denied me anything; He has never turned me away empty. He is such a wonderful Savior, such a Friend that we can depend upon with assurance and rest and complete confidence. He can roll away every burden. This afternoon think of Him as the exhaustless Savior, the everlasting Friend, One who knows all things, One who is able to help and deliver us. When we have such a Source as this, we can stretch out our hands and take all that we need from Him.

I will speak to you from the 11th chapter of Mark's gospel.

And Jesus entered into Jerusalem, and into the temple: and when he had looked round about upon all things, and now the eventide was come, he went out unto Bethany with the twelve. And on the morrow, when they were come from Bethany, he was hungry: and seeing a fig tree afar off having leaves, he came, if haply he might find anything thereon: and when he came to it, he found nothing but leaves; for the time of figs was not yet. And Jesus answered and said unto it, No man eat fruit of thee hereafter for ever. And his disciples heard it.

Mark 11:11-14

The fig tree dried up from the roots. We may think we have faith in God, but we must not doubt in our hearts, "...What things soever ye desire, when ye pray, believe that ye receive them, and ye shall have them" (Mark 11:24). This is a very wonderful word.

You meet here every Monday, and the great theme of this meeting is the theme of faith, so I will talk about faith. Your inactivity must be brought to a place of victory. Inactivity—that which wavers, that which hesitates, that which fears instead of having faith; that closes up everything, because it doubts instead of believing God. What is faith? Faith is the living principle of the Word of God. It is life, it produces life, it changes life.

Oh, that God today might give us a real knowledge of the Book. What is there in it? There is life. God wants us to feed on the Book, the living Word, the precious Word of God. All the wonderful things that Jesus did were done that people might be changed and made like unto Himself. Oh, to be like Him in thought, act, and plan. He went about His Father's business and was eaten up with the zeal of His house. I am beginning to understand First John 3:2:

Beloved, now are we the sons of God, and it doth not yet appear what we shall be: but we know that, when he shall appear, we shall be like him; for we shall see him as he is.

1 John 3:2

As I feed on the Word of God, my whole body will be changed by the process of the power of the Son of God.

But if the Spirit of him that raised up Jesus from the dead dwell in you, he that raised up Christ from the dead shall also quicken your mortal bodies by his Spirit that dwelleth in you.

Romans 8:11

The Lord dwells in a humble and contrite heart, and makes His way into the dry places, so if you open up to Him, He will flood you with His life, but be sure to remember that a little bit of sin will spoil a whole life. You can never cleanse sin, you can never purify sin, you can never be strong if in sin, you will never have a vision while in sin. Revelation stops when sin comes in. The human spirit must come to an end, but the Spirit of Christ must be alive and active. You must die to the human spirit, and then God will quicken your mortal body and make it alive. Without holiness no man shall see God (Heb. 12:14).

We have a wonderful subject. What is it? Faith. Faith is an inward operation of that divine power which dwells in the contrite heart, and which has power to lay hold of the things not seen. Faith is a divine act, faith is God in the soul. God operates by His Son, and transforms the natural into the supernatural. Faith is active, never dormant; faith lays hold, faith is the hand of God, faith is the power of God, faith never fears, faith lives amid the greatest conflict, faith is always active, faith moves even things that cannot be moved. God fills us with His divine power, and sin is dethroned. "The just shall live by faith" (Hab. 2:4; Rom. 1:17; Gal. 3:11; Heb. 10:38). You cannot live by faith until you are just (righteous). You cannot live by faith if you are unholy, or dishonest.

The Lord was looking for fruit on the tree. He found "nothing but leaves." There are thousands of people like that. They dress up like Christians, but it is all leaves. "Herein is my Father glorified, that ye bear much fruit..." (John 15:8). He has no way in which to get fruit, only through us. We have not to be ordinary people. To be saved is to be an extraordinary man, an exposition of God. When Jesus was talking about the new life He said, "...Except a man be born again [of God], he cannot see the kingdom of God. That which is born of the flesh is flesh; and that which is born of the Spirit is spirit" (John 3:3,6).

In order to understand His fullness we must be filled with the Holy Ghost. God has a measure for us that cannot be measured. I am invited into this measure; the measure of the Lord Jesus Christ in me. When you are in relationship, sin is dethroned, but you cannot purify yourself; it is by the blood of Jesus Christ, God's Son, that you are cleansed from all sin.

When Jesus saw nothing but leaves, He said to this tree: "No man eat fruit of thee hereafter for ever. And his disciples heard it" (Mark 11:14). The next morning as they passed the same place, they saw the fig tree dried up from the roots. You never see a tree dry from the roots. Even a little plant will dry from the top. But God's Son had spoken to the tree, and it could not live. He said to them, "Have faith in God" (Mark 11:22). We are His life, we are members of His body; the Spirit is in us, and there is no way to abide in the secret place of the Lord only by holiness.

Be filled with the Word of God. "For the word of God is quick, and powerful, and sharper than any twoedged sword, piercing even to the dividing asunder of soul and spirit..." (Heb. 4:12). Listen, those of you who have stiff knees and stiff arms today, you can get a tonic by the Word of God that will loosen your joints, and that will divide asunder even your joints and marrow. You cannot move your knee if there is not any marrow there, but the Word of God can bring marrow into your bones.

Anything else? One of the greatest things in the Word of God is that it discerns the thoughts and intents of the heart. Oh, that you may all allow the Word of God to have perfect victory in your body, so that it may be tingling through and through with God's divine power. Divine life does not belong to this world but to the kingdom of heaven, and the kingdom of heaven is within you. God wants to purify our minds until we can bear all things, believe all things, hope all things, and endure all things. God dwells in you, but you cannot have this divine power until you live and walk in the Holy Ghost, until the power of the new life is greater than the old life.

Jesus said to His disciples, if ye will believe in your heart not only the tree will wither but the mountain shall be removed. God wants us to move mountains. Anything that appears to be like a mountain can be moved. The mountains of difficulty, the mountains of perplexity, the mountains of depression or depravity. Things that bound you for years. Sometimes things appear as though they could not be moved, but you believe in your heart, stand on the Word of God, and God's Word will never be defeated.

Notice again this Scripture: "...What things soever ye desire, when ye pray, believe that ye receive them, and ye shall have them" (Mark 11:24). First, believe that you get them, and then you shall have them. That is the difficulty with people. They say: "Well, if I could feel I had it, I would know I had it," but you must believe it, and then the feeling will come; you must believe it because of the Word of God. God wants to work in you a real heart-faith.

I want you to know this afternoon that God has a real remedy for all your ailments. There is power in this meeting this afternoon to set everybody free.

Published in *Triumphs of Faith*

Wigglesworth walking the family dog

THE LAUGH OF FAITH
November 1930

My faith pure, my joy sure.

Romans 4

In Isaac (laughter) shall thy seed be called. Faith is the great inheritance, for the just shall live by faith. Twenty-five years Abraham waited for God to fulfill His promise to give him a son. He looked to God Who never fails, and believed His Word. As we live in the Spirit, we live in the process of God's mind, and act according to His will.

Could a child be born? Yes!! On the law of faith in God who had promised. Here is no limitation (Rom. 4:16). Therefore it is of faith, that it might be of grace. Grace is God's inheritance in the soul that believes.

Faith always brings a fact and a fact brings joy.

Faith! Faith! Making us know God is, and that He is a rewarder of those who diligently seek Him. God! Who quickeneth that which was dead, and calleth the things that are not as though they were. There is no want to those who trust God. He quickeneth the dead. The more Abraham was pressed, the more he rejoiced. Being not weak in faith. He considered not his own body. He staggered not through unbelief, but was strong in faith, giving glory to God, that what He had promised He was able to perform. Heir of the world through a righteousness by faith. God quickening that which is dead. The more there was no hope Abraham believed in hope. If we knew the value of trial we should praise God for it. It is in the furnace of affliction God gets us to the place where He can use us (Phil. 1:19). Paul says of difficulty, I do and will rejoice. For I know that this shall turn to my salvation through your prayers and the supply of the Spirit of Jesus Christ—that Christ shall be magnified in my body. Before God puts you in the furnace He knows you will go through. It is never above we are able to bear. If you know the baptism of the Holy Ghost is in the Scriptures, never rest until God gives it to you. If you know it is Scriptural to be healed of every weakness—to be holy, pure, to overcome amid all conditions—never rest until you are an overcomer.

If you have seen the face of God and have had vision and revelation, never rest until you attain to it. That ye may apprehend with all saints. Holy men spake as God gave them power and utterance. We must be blameless amid the crooked positions of the world. Jesus is the type of Sonship for our attainment. He was God's pattern, a firstfruit clothed with power. We must go in His name, that when you lay hands on the sick, satan has no power, and when you command in Jesus' name he has to go.

The walls are falling down,
The walls are falling down;
Oh praise the Lord. Praise ye His name,
The walls are falling down.

Let us take God's Word and stand upon it, as our strength to resist the devil till he is forced to flee. Amen, amen.

Published in *Redemption Tidings*

THE 'MUCH MORE' OF FAITH
June 15, 1935

In Romans 4:16 we read, "...it is of faith, that it might be by grace," meaning that we can open the door and God will come in. What will happen if we really open the door by faith? God is greater than our thoughts. He puts it to us, "...exceeding abundantly above all that we ask or think..." (Eph. 3:20). When we ask a lot, God says "more." Are we ready for the "more"? And then the "much more"? We may be, or we may miss it. We may be so endued by the Spirit of the Lord in the morning that it shall be a tonic for the whole day. God can so thrill us with new life that nothing ordinary or small will satisfy us after that. There is a great place for us in God where we won't be satisfied with small things. We won't have any satisfaction unless the fire falls, and whenever we pray we will have the assurance that what we have prayed for is going to follow the moment we open our mouth. Oh, this praying in the Spirit! This great plan of God for us! In a moment we can go right in. In where? Into His will. Then all things will be well.

You can't get anything asleep these days. The world is always awake, and we should always be awake to what God has for us. Awake to take! Awake to hold it after we get it! How much can you take? We know that God is more willing to give than we are to receive. How shall we dare to be asleep when the Spirit commands us to take everything on the table. It is the greatest banquet that ever was and ever will be—the table where all you take only leaves more behind. A fullness that cannot be exhausted! How many are prepared for a lot?

> *And Jesus entered into Jerusalem, and into the temple: and when he had looked round about upon all things, and now the eventide was come, he went out unto Bethany with the twelve. And on the morrow, when they were come from Bethany, he was hungry: And seeing a fig tree afar off having leaves; he came, if haply he might find any thing thereon: and when he came to it, he found nothing but leaves; for the time of figs was not yet. And Jesus answered and said unto it, No man eat fruit of thee hereafter for ever. And his disciples heard it.*
>
> *Mark 11:11-14*

Jesus was sent from God to meet the world's need. Jesus lived to minister life by the words He spoke, He said to Philip, "...he that hath seen me hath seen the Father...the words that I speak unto you I speak not of myself: but the Father that dwelleth in me..." (John 14:9,10). I am persuaded that if we are filled with His words of life and the Holy Ghost, and Christ is made manifest in our mortal flesh, then the Holy Ghost can really move us with His life, His words, till as He was, so are we in the world. We are receiving our life from God, and it is always kept in tremendous activity, working in our whole nature as we live in perfect contact with God.

Jesus spoke, and everything He said must come to pass. That is the great plan. When we are filled only with the Holy Spirit, and we won't allow the Word of God to be detracted by what we hear or by what we read, then comes the inspiration, then the life, then the activity, then the glory! Oh, to live in it! To live in it is to be moved by it. To live in it is to be moved so that we will have God's life, God's personality in the human body.

By the grace of God I want to impart the Word, and bring you into a place where you will dare to act upon the plan of the Word, to so breathe life by the power of the Word that it is impossible for you to go on under any circumstances without His provision. The most difficult things that come to us are to our advantage from God's side. When we come to the place of impossibilities it is the grandest place for us to see the possibilities of God. Put this right in your mind and never forget it. You will never be of any importance to God till you venture in the impossible. God wants people on the daring line. I do not mean foolish daring. "Be filled with the Spirit," and when we are filled with the Spirit we are not so much concerned about the secondary thing. It is the first with God.

Everything of evil, everything unclean, everything satanic in any way, is an objectionable thing to God, and we are to live above it, destroy it, not to allow it to have any place. Jesus didn't let the devil answer back. We must reach the place where we will not allow anything to interfere with the plan of God.

Jesus and His disciples came to the tree. It looked beautiful. It had the appearance of fruit, but when He came to it He found nothing but leaves. He was very disappointed. Looking at the tree, He spoke to it. Here is shown forth His destructive power, "...no man eat fruit of thee hereafter for ever" (Mark 11:14). The next day they were passing by the same way and the disciples saw the tree "...dried up from the roots" (Mark 11:20). They said to Jesus, "...behold, the fig tree which thou cursedst is withered away" (Mark 11:21). And Jesus said, "Have faith in God" (Mark 11:22).

There isn't a person who has ever seen a tree dried from the root. Trees always show the first signs of death right at the top. But the Master had spoken. The Master dealt with a natural thing to reveal to these disciples a supernatural plan. If He spoke, it would have to obey. And God, the Holy Ghost, wants us to understand clearly that we are the mouthpiece of God and are here for His divine plan. We may allow the natural mind to dethrone that, but in the measure we do, we won't come into the treasure which God has for us. The Word of God must have first place. It must not have a second place. In any measure that we doubt the Word of God, from that moment we have ceased to thrive spiritually and actively. The Word of God is not only to be looked at and read, but received as the Word of God to become life right within our life. "Thy word have I hid in mine heart, that I might not sin against thee" (Ps. 119:11).

"...I give unto you power...over all the power of the enemy..." (Luke 10:19). There it is. We can accept or reject it. I accept and believe it. It is a word beyond all human calculation. "Have faith in God." These disciples were in the Master's school. They were the men who were to turn the world upside down. As we receive the Word we will never be the same; if we dare to act as the Word goes forth and not be afraid, then God will honor us. "The Lord of hosts is with us; the God of Jacob is our refuge" (Ps. 46:7). Jacob was the weakest of all, in any way you like to take it. He is the God of Jacob, and He is our God. So we may likewise have our names changed to Israel.

As the Lord Jesus injected this wonderful Word, "Have faith in God," into the disciples, He began to show how it was to be. Looking around about Him He saw the mountains, and He began to bring a practical application.

A truth means nothing unless it moves us. We can have our minds filled 1,000 times, but it must get into our hearts if there are to be any results. All inspiration is in the heart. All compassion is in the heart.

Looking at the mountains He said, "Shall not doubt in his heart." That is the barometer. You know exactly where you are. The man knows when he prays. If his heart is right how it leaps. No man is any good for God and never makes progress in God who does not hate sin. You are never safe. But there is a place in God where you can love righteousness and where you can hate iniquity till the Word of God is a light in your bosom, quickening every fiber of your body, thrilling your whole nature. The pure in heart see God. Believe in the heart! What a word! If I believe in my heart God says I can begin to speak, and "whatsoever" I say shall come to pass.

Here is an act of believing in the heart. I was called to Halifax, England, to pray for a lady missionary. I found it an urgent call. I could see there was an absence of faith, and I could see there was death. Death is a terrible thing, and God wants to keep us alive. I know it is appointed unto man once to die, but I believe in a rapturous death. I said to the woman, "How are you?" She said, "I have faith," in a very weak tone of voice. "Faith? Why you are dying? Brother Walshaw, is she dying?" "Yes." To a friend standing by, "Is she dying?" "Yes."

Now I believe there is something in a heart that is against defeat, and this is the faith which God hath given to us. I said to her, "In the name of Jesus, now believe and you'll live." She said, "I believe," and God sent life from her head to her feet. They dressed her and she lived.

"Have faith." It isn't *saying* you have faith. It is he that *believeth in his heart*. It is a grasping of the eternal God. Faith is God in the human vessel. "...this is the victory that overcometh the world, even our faith" (1 John 5:4). He that believeth *overcomes* the world. "...faith cometh by hearing, and hearing by the word of God" (Rom. 10:17). He that believeth in his heart! Can you imagine anything easier than that? He that believeth in his heart! What is the process? Death! No one can live who believes in his heart. He dies to everything worldly. He that loves the world is not of God. You can measure the whole thing up, and examine yourself to see if you have faith. Faith is a life. Faith enables you to lay hold of that which is and get it out of the way for God to bring in something that is not.

Just before I left home I was in Norway. A woman wrote to me from England saying she had been operated on for cancer three years before, but that it was now coming back. She was living in constant dread of the whole thing as the operation was so painful. Would it be possible to see me when I returned to England? I wrote that I would be passing through London on the 20th of June last year. If she would like to meet me at the hotel I would pray for her. She replied that she would be going to London to be there to meet me. When I met this woman I saw she was in great pain, and I have great sympathy for people who have tried to get relief and have failed. If you preachers lose your compassion you can stop preaching, for it won't be any good. You will only be successful as a preacher as you let your heart become filled with the compassion of Jesus. As soon as I saw her I entered into the state of her mind. I saw how distressed she was. She came to me in a mournful spirit, and her whole face was downcast. I said to her, "There are two things going to happen today. One is that you are to know that you are saved." "Oh, if I could only know I was saved," she said. "There is another thing. You have to go out of this hotel without a pain, without a trace of the cancer."

Then I began with the Word. Oh, this wonderful Word! We do not have to go up to bring Him down; neither do we have to go down to bring Him up. "...the word is nigh thee, even in thy mouth, and in thy heart: that is, the word of faith, which we preach" (Rom. 10:8). I said, "Believe that He took your sins when He died at the cross. Believe that when He was buried, it was for you. Believe that when He arose, it was for you. And now at God's right hand He is sitting for you. If you can believe in your heart and confess with your mouth, you shall be saved." She looked at me saying, "Oh, it is going all through my body. I know I am saved now. If He comes today, I'll go. How I have dreaded the thought of His coming all my life! But if He comes today, I know I shall be ready."

The first thing was finished. Now for the second. I laid my hands upon her in the name of Jesus, believing in my heart that I could say what I wanted and it should be done. I said, "In the name of Jesus, I cast this out." She jumped up. "Two things have happened," she said. "I am saved and now the cancer is gone."

Faith will stand amid the wrecks of time,
Faith unto eternal glories climb;
Only count the promise true,
And the Lord will stand by you.
Faith will win the victory *every* time!

So many people have nervous trouble. I'll tell you how to get rid of your nervous trouble. I have something in my bag, one dose of which will cure you. "...I am the Lord that healeth thee" (Exod. 15:26). How this wonderful Word of God changes the situation. "...perfect love casteth out fear..." (1 John 4:18). "There is no fear in love..." (1 John 4:18). I have tested that so often, casting out the whole condition of fear and the whole situation has been changed. We have a big God, only He has to be absolutely and only trusted. The people who really do believe God are strong, and "...he that hath clean hands shall be stronger and stronger" [Job17:9]

At the close of a certain meeting a man said to me, "You have helped everybody but me. I wish you would help me." "What's the trouble with you?" "I cannot sleep because of nervous trouble. My wife says she has not known me to have a full night's sleep for three years. I am just shattered." Anyone could tell he was. I put my hands upon him and said, "Brother, I believe in my heart. Go home and sleep in the name of Jesus." "I can't sleep." "Go home and sleep in the name of Jesus." "I can't sleep." The lights were being put out, and I took the man by the coat collar and said, "Don't talk to me anymore." That was sufficient. He went after that. When he got home his mother and wife said to him, "What has happened?" "Nothing. He helped everybody but me." "Surely he said something to you." "He told me to come home and sleep in the name of Jesus, but you know I can't sleep in anything."

His wife urged him to do what I had said, and he had scarcely got his head on the pillow before the Lord put him to sleep. The next morning he was still asleep. She began to make a noise in the bedroom to awaken him, but he did not waken. Sunday morning he was still asleep. She did what every good wife would do. She decided to make a good Sunday dinner, and then awaken him. After the dinner was prepared she went up to him and put her hand on his shoulder and shook him, saying, "Are you never going to wake up?" From that night that man never had any more nervousness.

A man came to me for whom I prayed. Then I asked, "Are you sure you are perfectly healed?" "Well," he said, "there is just a little pain in my shoulder." "Do you know what that is?" I asked him. "That is unbelief. Were you saved before you believed or after?" "After." "You will be healed after." "It is all right now," he said. It was all right before, but he hadn't believed.

The Word of God is for us. It is by faith that it might be by grace.

Published in *The Pentecostal Evangel*

THE LIFE THAT VENTURES ON THE WORD OF GOD

September 11, 1936

God has drawn us together and He has something to give us. He is not ordinary, but extraordinary, not measured, but immeasurable, abounding in everything. There is nothing small about our God, and when we understand God we will find out that there ought not to be anything small about us. We must have

An Enlargement of Our Conception of God,

then we will know that we have come to a place where all things are possible, for our God is an omnipotent God for impossible positions.

We are born into a family that never dies, and it is the plan of God to subdue all things that are natural to a supernatural order. Nothing about us has to be dwarfed. God comes in with His mighty power and so works in us that sin has no dominion; evil is subdued, and God's Son begins to reign on the throne of your heart, transforming that which was weak and helpless.

But there must be a revolution if we would have almighty God living in and controlling our mortal flesh. We must conclude that there is no good thing in the flesh, and then we must know that God can come in the flesh and subject it till every mighty thing can be manifested through the human order.

Now, beloved, have you come for a blessing? Turn to Hebrews, chapter 11.

The Christian life is a going-on, a non-stop, until you reach the top. If you ever stop between Calvary and the glory, it is you who blocked the way. There is no stop between Calvary and the glory except by human failure, but if you allow God to have His way, He will surely transform us, for His plan is to change us from what we are to what He intends us to be, and never to lose the ideal of His great plan for us. God wants to shake us loose and take the cobwebs away, and remove all the husks from the wheat, that we may be pure grain for God to work upon. In order to do that we must be willing to let go; as long as you hold on to the natural, you cannot take hold of divine life.

The child of God has never to be on the line of speculation but on the line of faith, with audacity to prove that God is what He has promised to be. You will not get strong in faith until you

VENTURE ON THE IMPOSSIBLE.

If you ask for anything six times, five is unbelief. You are not heard for your much speaking, but because you believe. If you pray round the world, you will get into a whirlwind, and spoil every meeting you get into.

Now God does not want anybody in the world, under any circumstances, to be in a place where they live on eyesight and on feelings. Faith never feels and faith never looks. Faith is an act, and faith without an act is not faith, but doubt and disgrace. Every one of you has more faith than you are using.

Now this "substance" I am speaking about cannot be looked at nor handled. God wants us to have something greater than what we can see and handle. It is declared in the Scriptures that the earth is going to be melted with fervent heat and the heavens shall depart, but the Word will remain, and this is substance. So we must know whether we are living in substance that cannot be handled or living in the temporal, for everything you can see is going to be moved, and that which you cannot see is going to remain forever.

God gives us this remarkable substance that is called faith. It consists of the Word of God, of the personality of God, of the nature of God, and the acts of God, and those four things are all in faith. Faith is a deep reality caused by God's personality waking up our humanity to leap into eternal things and be lost forever in something a million times greater than yourself. To be possessed by and be the possessor of something a million times greater than you!

THERE IS ALWAYS A GOING-ON WITH GOD.

There is a growing in faith after we are saved. Backsliding is knowing the way of holiness and shutting the door. So if you know to do good and you do not do it, that is backsliding. What standard is holiness? There is none. A person who is newborn is as holy as the aged while he walks according to the light he has, and the oldest saint with more light is not more holy than the person who is just saved and walking in the light.

You cannot make anything without material, but I want to read to you of something being made without material.

Through faith we understand that the worlds were framed by the word of God, so that things which are seen were not made of things which do appear.

Hebrews 11:3

God took the Word and made this world out of things that were not there. He caused it all to come by the word of faith. You were born of, created by, made anew by, the same word that made the world. God, in His infinite mercy, brings His infinite light and power right into our finite being so that we have revelations of the mighty God and of His wonderful power. That is the reason why I lay hands on the sick and know they will be healed.

God has taken all ranks and conditions of people to make the 11th chapter of Hebrews. Samson made terrible mistakes, but he is included. Then there is Barak who wouldn't go without Deborah. He couldn't have been a strong man when a woman had to go with him, but he is mentioned. Now why can you not believe that God will have you also included.

The Acts of the Apostles finishes abruptly. It is not finished, and all who are in this place tonight must add to the Acts of the Apostles. This is a record of an incompletion, because when you get there you will find you are among the Acts of the Apostles.

WATCH THAT NOBODY TAKES YOUR CROWN.

You have to be zealous. You have not to let anybody stand in your way. Salvation is the beginning; sanctification is a continuation; the baptism in the Holy Ghost is the enlargement of capacity for the risen Christ. God comes along and inspires your thoughts and says, "Now go forward, My child; it will be all right. Do not give in."

The Lord may permit your tire to be punctured many a time, but you must not be discouraged because the wind has gone out. You must pump it up again. The life that He began cannot be taken away from you. If you have an inspiration to "go forth," you cannot be stopped. You know you are called to an eternal purpose and nothing shall stand in your way. It is His purpose that we shall be sanctified, purified, and renewed. We are a people who have been raised from the dead, and if Jesus comes, you go because you have resurrection in you.

The elders always had a good report because of faith, and if devastating winds blow, it does not matter. The men of faith are not moved by anything they see or hear. The man of faith does not live in time. He has begun in eternity. He does not count on the things that are;

HE RELIES ON THE THINGS THAT ARE NOT.

We must be in the place of buoyancy. The man of faith is subject to God, but never in subjection to the devil. He is not puffed up. No, he lives in meekness and grows in grace. If you ask God to give you power, you have fallen from grace. You have power after the Holy Ghost is come upon you. Act in faith. Act in wisdom, "For it is God which worketh in you both to will and to do of his good pleasure" (Phil. 2:13).

Published in *Redemption Tidings*

HEAVENLY INTOXICATION
August 13, 1937

The divine plan is so much greater than all human thought. When He can only have us in His hand, when we are willing to yield to His sovereign will, when we have no reserve, how wonderful God is, always willing to open the door till our whole life is filled with the fragrance of heaven. Heaven is right here, for Jesus is the substance and fullness of the divine nature, and He dwells in our hearts. Oh this wonderful fascinating Jesus, eating into our hearts and burning in our bosom. What a wonderful Jesus we have. Something about Him kindles fire in the darkest place. Something about our Lord makes all darkness light. God's Son is for all our human nature, and when we have Him we have more than we can speak about and think about. God's Son can set the world ablaze and bring heaven right into the place where we live. I am going to read Hebrews 11:5.

> *By faith Enoch was translated that he should not see death; and was not found, because God had translated him: for before his translation he had this testimony, that he pleased God.*
>
> *Hebrews 11:5*

THE DISPENSATION OF THE HOLY GHOST

Without faith it is impossible to please God, and he that cometh to God must believe that God is, and that God is working, able to work out the plan, and is working through you if you believe that God is. Possibilities are within your reach if you dare to believe that God is.

Evil spirits have no more control, if I believe that God is, and I do, I do. I know I am free from all the powers of darkness, free from all the powers of evil, and it is a wonderful thing to be free, and because you are free you step into the liberty of freed men and claim the possessions of God.

This is the dispensation of the Holy Ghost. It is 29 years ago since God filled me with the Holy Ghost, and it burned in my bosom and it is still burning, with more activity for God than 29 years ago. The Holy Spirit is not played out.

How God Moved

It will be ridiculous for me to begin to speak about myself in South Africa, but I think it is fair to say what they said and not Wigglesworth. At every place without exception the people said, "We have never seen anything like this before in our lives." When we arrived at Cape Town, people I had never seen before came running all around so, so glad to see us. One man threw his arms round me and kissed me, full of joy to see the man his heart had been longing for years. God is waiting for people who dare to believe, and when you believe all things are possible.

Only believe, Only believe,
All things are possible, Only believe.
Only believe, Only believe,
All things are possible, Only believe.

It is the breath of God. It is the Word of the Spirit. It is the revelation of the Most High. God wants to show you to sweep away everything else, and dare to believe that Word. If you allow anything to come in between you and that Word, it will poison your whole system, and you will have no hope. One bit of unbelief against that Word is poison. It is like the devil putting a spear into you. It is the Word of life. It is the breath of heaven. It is God and His breath of quickening power by which your very life is changed, and you begin to bear the image of the heavenly. The people said, "We are ready for you." We began the same night. A man was there whose deathly face was filled with the very devil's manifestation of cancer. I said to the people, "Here is a man in the place suffering with a tremendous thing. He does not know I am talking about him at all. You can have the choice, if you desire me to deliver that man, so as to enjoy the meeting, I will go down in the name of the Lord and deliver him, or I will preach." They said, "Come down." I went down and the people saw what God had done and saw that man shouting, raving, for he was like a man that was intoxicated. He was shouting, "I am free, I have been unbound." They were getting all the cameras ready and there was flash after flash. It was a wonderful thing to see that man changed. It was wonderful how God sustained me in the heat, wet through. The people said at the end of the campaign that we ought to have some rest, and yet there we were fresh to go on, ready to make other people dare to believe God. You cannot measure our conditions. They are immeasurable. Divine association with God is more than ten regiments of soldiers. Jesus said, "I will pray the Father to send legions of angels." We must pray tonight that God will send us a deluge. It shall be unto you if you believe.

THE MANIFESTATION OF FAITH

One man after laying out £900 upon his dear wife for operation after operation, year by year, brought her helpless to the meeting. Now I knew for a fact that nothing could help that woman, only after seeing acts of faith. I went to her and said, "Look here, this is the greatest opportunity of your life. You will see that I will give an altar call tonight. There will be 50 people come up, and when you see them loosed, you believe, and you will be loosed like them, and then we will have a testimony from you." They came and my hands were laid upon them in the name of the Lord and I said "testify" and they testified. This woman saw their faces, and when all these people were through I said, "Do you believe?" and she said "I cannot help but believe." There is something in the manifestation of faith. I laid hands upon her in the name of Jesus and the power of God went right through her. I said, "In the name of Jesus, arise and walk." An impossibility! If you do not venture, you remain ordinary as long as you live. If you dare the impossible then God will abundantly do far above all you can ask or think. As if a cannon had blown her up, she rose and I thought her husband would go mad with joy and excitement because he saw his wife mightily moved by the power of God, made free, the first in the meeting afterward to glorify God.

HEAVENLY INTOXICATION

My brethren, this is reality that I am talking about. It burns in my bones, it thrills my whole being. My whole being is blessed with the intoxication of heaven.

The first meeting the fire broke out. The people were standing out in the streets, and we went to the town hall and over 1,000 people were saved by the power of God. They were so intoxicated by the thing that was shown that the first Sunday after we went, over 300 met together.

A young man read my book, who was dying of consumption, and he was saved and then God healed him. Then this young man so grew in the knowledge of God, he was made a pastor, and he came up to me like a son to a father. "If you like, I will go with you all the way over South Africa." He had had a wonderful education, and we said we will let him go all the way. He bought the best car for the job. If you go to South Africa you must have a car to go through the ploughed fields, one that will jump the hedges, jump in the river, and jump out again. That young man drove us 5,000 miles through all the territories, right amongst the Zulus, and rode in every place and God took us through everything. Talk about life, why this is overcoming life.

If there is anyone in this meeting who wants to be saved, this is your opportunity, and I will pray for you. There is a man who wants to be saved. Thank God. God will answer prayer for that man. There is a young man down there. God bless you. Who is the next? Here is a young woman who wants to be saved. Is there another now? Come now, do not fail to take this opportunity.

A sermon preached by Smith Wigglesworth at Sion College
on April 16th after his return from his South African Tour

Published in *Redemption Tidings*

A POWER, BEYOND
AND WITHIN

December 1941

Hebrews 11:1-6. You know, beloved, that there are many wonderful treasures in the storehouse of God that we have not yet gotten. But praise God, we have the promise in Corinthians:

> *...Eye hath not seen, nor ear heard, neither have entered into the heart of man, the things which God hath prepared for them that love him.*
>
> *1 Corinthians 2:9*

I pray God that there may be within us a deep hunger and thirst with the penetration which is centered entirely upon the axle of Him, for surely He is all and in all. I pray God that we may be able to understand the opening of this chapter.

A REAL FOUNDATION

Now, beloved, you will clearly see that God wants to bring us to a foundation. If we are ever going to make any progress in divine life we shall have to have a real foundation. And there is no foundation, only the foundation of faith for us.

All our movements, and all that ever will come to us, which is of any importance, will be because we have a *Rock*. And if you are on the Rock, no powers can move you. And the need of today is the Rock to have our faith firm upon.

On any line or principle of your faith you must have something established in you to bring that forth. And there is no establishment outside God's Word for you. Everything else is sand. Everything else shall sunder.

If you build on anything else but the Word of God—on imaginations, sentimentality, or any feelings, or any special joy, it will mean nothing without you have a foundation, and the foundation will have to be in the Word of God.

We must have something better than sand, and everything is sand except the Word. There isn't anything that will remain—we are told the heaven and earth will be melted up as a scroll as fervent heat. But we are told the Word of God shall be forever, and not one jot or tittle of the Word of God shall fail. And if there is anything that is satisfying me today more than another, it is, "Thy Word is settled in heaven."

And another word in the 138th Psalm says: "...thou hast magnified thy word above all thy name" (Ps. 138:2). The very establishment for me is the Word of God. It is not on any other line. Let us come to the principle of it. If you turn to John's gospel you will find a wonderful word there. It is worth our notice and great consideration.

In the beginning was the Word, and the Word was with God, and the Word was God. The same was in the beginning with God. All things were made by him; and without him was not any thing made that was made.

John 1:1-3

THE WORD

There we have the foundation of all things, which is the Word. It is a substance. It is a power. It is more than relationship. It is personality. It is a divine injunction to every soul that enters into this privilege to be born of this Word. What it means to us will be very important for us. For remember, it is a substance, it is an evidence of things not seen. It bringeth about that which you cannot see. It brings forth that which is not there, and takes away that that is there, and substitutes it. God took the Word and made the world of the things which did not appear. And we live in the world which was made by the Word of God, and it is inhabited by millions of people. And you say it is a substance. Jesus, the Word of God, made it of the things which did not appear. And there is not anything made that is made that has not been made by the Word. And when we come to the truth of what that Word means, we shall be able not only to build but to know, not only to know, but to have. For if there is anything helping me today more than another, it is the fact that I am living in facts, I am moving in facts, I am in the knowledge of the principles of the Most High.

God is making manifest His power. God is a reality and proving His mightiness in the midst of us. And as we open ourselves to divine revelation and get rid of all things that are not of the Spirit, then we shall understand how mightily God can take us on in the Spirit, and move the things which are, and bring the things which are not into prominence. Oh, the riches, the depths of the wisdom of the Most High God! May this morning enlarge us. Jabus knew that there were divine principles that we need to know, and he says, "Enlarge me."

David knew that there was a mightiness beyond and within, and he says, "Thou has dealt bountifully with me," knowing that all the springs came from God that were in Him which made His face to shine.

And God is an inward witness of a power, of a truth, of a revelation, of an inward presence, of a divine knowledge. He is! He is!

Then I must understand. I must clearly understand. I must have a basis of knowledge for everything that I say. We must, as preachers, never preach what we think. We must say what we know. Any man can think. You must be beyond the thinking. You must be in the teaching. You must have the knowledge. And God wants to make us so in fidelity with Him that He unveils Himself. He rolls the clouds away, the mists disappear at His presence. He is almighty in His movements.

God has nothing small. He is all large, immensity of wisdom, unfolding the grandeur of His design or plan for humanity, that humanity may sink into insignificance, and the mightiness of the mighty power of God may move upon us till we are the sons of God with power, in revelation, and might and strength in the knowledge of God.

THE PRINCIPLE OF GOD

I think John has a wonderful word on this which is to edify at this moment—very powerful in its revelation to me so often as I gaze into the perfect law of liberty.

Let me read from the First Epistle of John:

That which was from the beginning, which we have heard, which we have seen with our eyes, which we have looked upon, and our hands have handled, of the Word of life; (For the life was manifested, and we have seen it, and bear witness, and show unto you that eternal life, which was with the Father, and was manifested unto us;) That which we have seen and heard declare we unto you, that ye also may have fellowship with us: and truly our fellowship is with the Father, and with his Son Jesus Christ.

1 John 1:1-3

Oh beloved, He is the Word! He is the principle of God. He is the revelation sent forth from God. All fullness dwelt in Him. This is a grand word, of His fullness we have all received, and grace for grace.

In weakness, strength. In poverty, wealth. Oh, brother, this Word! It is a flame of fire. It may burn in your bones. It may move in every tissue of your life. It may bring out of you so forcibly the plan and purpose and life of God, till you cease to be, for God has taken you.

It is a fact we may be taken, hallelujah! into all the knowledge of the wisdom of God. Then I want to build, if I am created anew, for it is a great creation. It took nine months to bring us forth into the world after we were conceived, but it only takes one moment to beget us as sons. The first formation was a long period of nine months. The second formation is a moment, is an act, is a faith, for "He that believeth hath." And as you receive Him, you are begotten, not made.

Oh, the fact that I am begotten again, wonderful! Begotten of the same seed that begot Him. Remember, as He was conceived in the womb by the Holy Ghost, so we were conceived the moment we believed and became in a principle of the like-mindedness of an open door to become sons of God with promise.

Sons must have power. We must have power with God, power with man. We must be above all the world. We must have power over satan, power over the evils. I want you just for a moment to think with me because it will help you with this thought.

You can never make evil pure. Anything which is evil never becomes pure in that sense. There is no such a thing as ever creating impurity into purity. The carnal mind is never subject to the will of God, and cannot be. There is only one thing. It must be destroyed.

But I want you to go with me to when God cast out that which was not pure. I want you to think about satan in the glory with all the chances, and nothing spoiled him but his pride. And pride is an awful thing. Pride in the heart, thinking we are something when we are nothing. Building up a human constitution out of our own.

Oh yes, it is true the devil is ever trying to make you think what you are. You never find God doing it. It is always satan who comes on and says, "What a wonderful address you gave! How wonderful he did that, and how wonderful he prayed, and sang that song." It is all of the devil. There is not an atom of God in it, not from beginning to end.

VISION DAY BY DAY

Oh, the vision is so needy today, more needy than anything that man should have the visions of God. The people have always perished when there is no vision. God wants us to have visions and revelations and manifestations.

You cannot have the Holy Ghost without having revelations. You cannot have the Holy Ghost without being turned into another nature. It was the only credential by which Joshua and Caleb could enter the land because they were of another spirit.

And we must live in an unction, in a power, in a transformation, and a divine attainment where we cease to be, where God becomes enthroned so richly.

"It is He! He came forth, emptied Himself of all, but love brought to us the grace and then offered up Himself to purge us that we might be entire and free from all things. That we should see Him who was invisible, and changed by the power which is divine, and be lost to everything but the immensity of the mightiness of a godlikeness, for we must be in the world sons of God with promise."

We must be—we must be! We must not say it is not for me. Oh, no; we must say, "It is for us."

And God cast satan out. Oh, I do thank God for that. Yes, beloved, but God could not have cast him out if he had even been equal of power. I tell you, beloved, we can never bind the strong man till we are in the place of binding.

Thank God satan had to come out. Yes, and how did he come out? By the Word of His power. And, beloved, if we get to know and understand the principles of our inheritance by faith, we shall find out satan will always be cast out by the same power that cast him out in the beginning. He will be cast out to the end because satan has not become more holy but more vile.

If you think about the last day upon earth, you will find out that the greatest war—not Armageddon, the war beyond that—will be betwixt the hosts of satan and the hosts of God. And how will it take place? With swords, dynamite, or any human power? No! By the brightness of His presence, the holiness of His holiness, the purity of His purity, where darkness cannot remain, where sin cannot stand, where only holiness, purity will remain. All else will flee from the presence of God into the abyss forever.

And God has saved us with this Word of power over the powers of sin. I know there is a teaching and a need of teaching of the personality of the presence of the fidelity of the Word of God with power. And we need to eat and drink of this Word. We need to feed upon it in our hearts. We need that holy revelation that ought always to take away the mists from our eyes and reveal Him.

Remember, beloved, don't forget that every day must be a day of advancement. If you have not made any advancement since yesterday, in a measure you are a backslider. There is only one way for you between Calvary and the glory, and it is forward. It is every day forward. It is no day back. It is advancement with God. It is cooperation with Him in the Spirit.

Beloved, we must see these things, because if we live on the same plane day after day, the vision is stale, the principles lose their earnestness. But we must be like those who are catching the vision of the Master day by day. And we must make inroads into every passion that would interfere and bring everything to the slaughter that is not holy. For God would have us in these days to know that He wishes to seat us on high. Don't forget it.

The principles remain with us (if we will only obey) to seat us on high, hallelujah! And let us still go on building because we must build this morning. We must know our foundation. We must be able to take the Word of God and so make it clear to people because we shall be confronted with evil powers.

Reconstructed

I am continually confronted with things which God must clear away. Every day something comes before me that has to be dealt with on these lines. For instance, when I was at Cazadero seven or eight years ago, amongst the first people that came to me in those meetings was a man who was stone deaf. And every time we had the meeting—suppose I was rising up to say a few words, this man would take his chair from off the ordinary row and place it right in front of me. And the devil used to say, "Now, you are done." I said, "No, I am not done. It is finished."

The man was as deaf as possible for three weeks. And then in the meetings, as we were singing about three weeks afterward, this man became tremendously disturbed as though in a storm. He looked in every direction, and he became as one who had almost lost his mind. And then he took a leap. He started on the run and went out amongst the people, and right up one of the hills. When he got about 60 yards away he heard singing. And the Lord said, "Thy ears are open." And he came back, and we were still singing. That stopped our singing. And then he told us that when his ears were opened he could not understand what it was. There was such a tremendous noise he could not understand it whatever. He thought something had happened to the world, and so he ran out of the whole thing. Then, when he got away, he heard singing.

Oh, the devil said for three weeks, "You cannot do it." I said, "It is done!" As though God would ever forget! As though God could ever forget! As if it were possible for God to ever ignore our prayers!

145

The most trying time is the most helpful time. Most preachers say something about Daniel, and about the Hebrew children, and especially about Moses when he was in a tried corner. Beloved, if you read the Scriptures you will never find anything about the easy time. All the glories came out of hard times.

And if you are really reconstructed it will be in a hard time—it won't be in a singing meeting, but at a time when you think all things are dried up, when you think there is no hope for you, and you have passed everything, then that is the time that God makes the man, when tried by fire that God purges you, takes the dross away and brings forth the pure gold. Only melted gold is minted. Only moistened clay receives the mould. Only soft wax receives the seal. Only broken, contrite hearts receive the mark as the potter turns us on his wheel, shaped and burnt to take and keep the heavenly mould, the stamp of God's pure gold.

We must have the stamp of our blessed Lord, who was marred more than any man. And when He touched human weakness it was reconstructed. He spoke out of the depths of trial and mockery, and became the initiative of a world's redemption. Never man spoke like He spake! He was full of order and made all things move till they said, "We never saw it like this."

He is truly the Son of God with power, with blessing, with life, with maturity, and He can take the weakest and make them into strength.

Published in *Revival News*

TWO KINDS OF FAITH

April 21, 1945

We read in the Word that by faith Abel offered unto God a more excellent sacrifice than Cain; by faith Enoch was translated that he should not see death; by faith Noah prepared an ark to the saving of his house; by faith Abraham, when he was called to go out into a place which he should after receive for an inheritance, obeyed (Hebrews 11). There is only one way to all the treasures of God, and that is the way of faith. All things are possible, the fulfilling of all promises, to him that believeth. And it is all by grace.

...by grace are ye saved through faith; and that not of yourselves: it is the gift of God.

Ephesians 2:8

There will be failure in our lives if we do not build on the base, the Rock Christ Jesus. He is the only way. He is the truth. He is the life. And the Word He gives us is life-giving. As we receive the Word of life, it quickens, it opens, it fills us, it moves us, it changes us; and it brings us into a place where we dare to say amen to all that God has said. Beloved, there is a lot in an "Amen." You never get any place until you have the Amen inside of you. That was the difference between Zacharias and Mary. When the Word came to Zacharias he was filled with unbelief until the angel said, "thou shalt be dumb...because thou believest not my words..." (Luke 1:20). Mary said, "...be it unto me according to thy Word..." (Luke 1:38). And the Lord was pleased that she believed that there would be a performance. When we believe what God has said, *there shall be a performance.*

Read the 12th chapter of Acts, and you will find that there were people waiting all night and praying that Peter might come out of prison. But there seemed to be one thing missing despite all their praying, and that was faith. Rhoda had more faith than all the rest of them. When the knock came at the door, she ran to it for she was expecting an answer to her prayers; and the moment she heard Peter's voice, she ran back and announced to them that Peter was standing at the door. And all the people said, "You are mad. It isn't so." That was not faith. When she insisted that he was there, they said, "Well, perhaps God has sent his angel." But Rhoda insisted, "It is Peter." And Peter continued knocking. And they went out and found it so. What Rhoda had believed for had become a glorious fact.

Beloved, we may do much praying and groaning, but we do not receive from God because of that; we receive because we believe. And yet sometimes it takes God a long time to bring us through the groaning and the crying before we can believe.

I know this, that no man by his praying can change God—for you cannot change Him. Finney said, "Can a man who is full of sin and all kinds of ruin in his life, change God when he starts to pray?" No, it is impossible. But when a man labors in prayer, he groans and travails because his tremendous sin is weighing him down, and he becomes broken in the presence of God; and when properly melted he comes into perfect harmony with the divine plan of God, and then God can work in that clay. He could not before. Prayer changes hearts, but it never changes God. He is the same yesterday, and today, and forever—full of love, full of compassion, full of mercy, full of grace, and ready to bestow this and communicate that to us as we come in faith to Him.

Believe that when you come into the presence of God you can have all you came for. You can take it away; and you can use it, for all the power of God is at your disposal in response to your faith. The price for all was paid by the blood of Jesus Christ at Calvary. Oh, He is the living God, the One who has power to change us! "...it is he that hath made us, and not we ourselves..." (Ps. 100:3). And He purposes to transform us so that the greatness of His power may work through us. Oh, beloved! God delight in us, and when a man's ways please the Lord, then He makes all things to move according to His own blessed purpose.

We read in Hebrews 11:5, "By faith Enoch was translated that he should not see death...before his translation he had this testimony, that he pleased God." I believe it is in the mind of God to prepare us for translation. But remember this, translation comes only on the line of holy obedience and a walk according to the good pleasure of God. We are called to walk together with God through the Spirit. It is delightful to know that we can talk with God and hold communion with Him. Through this wonderful baptism in the Spirit which the Lord gives us, He enables us to talk to Himself in a language that the Spirit has given, a language which no man understands but which He understands, a language of love. Oh, how wonderful it is to speak to Him in the Spirit, to let the Spirit lift, and lift and lift us until He takes us into the very presence of God! I pray that God by His Spirit may move all of us so that we walk with God even as Enoch walked with Him. But beloved, it is a walk by faith and not by sight, a walk of believing the Word of God.

I believe there are two kinds of faith. All people are born with a natural faith but God calls us to a supernatural faith which is a gift from Himself. In the 26th chapter of Acts Paul tells us of his call, how God spoke to him and told him to go to the Gentiles, "To open their eyes, and to turn them from darkness to light, and from the power of Satan unto God, that they may receive forgiveness of sins, and inheritance among them which are sanctified by faith that is in me" (Acts 26:18). The faith which was in Christ was by the Holy Spirit to be given to those who believed. Henceforth, as Paul yielded his life to God, he could say,

I am crucified with Christ: nevertheless I live; yet not I, but Christ liveth in me: and the life which I now live in the flesh I live by the faith of the Son of God, who loved me, and gave himself for me.

Galatians 2:20

The faith of the Son of God communicated by the Spirit to the one who puts his trust in God and in His Son.

I want to show you the difference between our faith and the faith of Jesus. Our faith is limited and comes to an end. Most people have experienced coming to the place where they have said, "Lord, I can go no further. I have gone so far, and I cannot go on." But God can help us and take us beyond this. I remember one night, being in the north of England and going around to see some sick people, I was taken into a house where there was a young woman lying on her bed, a very helpless case. Her reason was gone and many things were manifested that were absolutely satanic, and I knew it.

She was a beautiful young woman. Her husband was quite a young man. He came in with a baby in his arms, leaned over and kissed his wife. The moment he did so she threw herself over on the other side of the bed, just as a lunatic would do, with no consciousness of the presence of her husband. It was heartbreaking. The husband took the baby and pressed the baby's lips to the mother. Again there was a wild frenzy. I said to the sister who was attending her, "Have you anybody to help?" She answered, "We have done everything we could." I said, "Have you no spiritual help?" Her husband stormed and said, "Spiritual help? Do you think we believe in God after we have had seven weeks of no sleep and this maniac condition? If you think we believe in God, you are mistaken. You have come to the wrong house."

There was a young woman about 18 who grinned at me as she passed out of the door, as much as to say, "You cannot do anything." But this brought me to a place of compassion for this poor young woman. And then with what faith I had I began to penetrate the heavens. I was soon out on the heights, and I tell you I never saw a man get anything from God who prayed on the earth level. If you get anything from God you will have to pray right into heaven, for all you want is there. If you are living an earthly life, all taken up with sensual things, and expect things from heaven, they will never come. God wants us to be a heavenly people, seated with Him in the heavenlies, and laying hold of all the things in heaven that are at our disposal.

I saw there, in the presence of that demented girl, limitations to my faith; but as I prayed there came another faith into my heart that could not be denied, a faith that grasped the promises, a faith that believed God's Word. I came from the presence of the glory back to earth. I was not the same man. I confronted the same conditions I had seen before, but in the name of Jesus. With a faith that could shake hell and move anything else, I cried to the demon power that was making this young woman a maniac, "Come out of her, in the name of Jesus!" She rolled over and fell asleep, and awakened in 14 hours, perfectly sane and perfectly whole.

Enoch walked with God. During those many years of his life he was penetrating the heavens, laying hold of and believing God, living with such cooperation and such a touch of God upon him that things moved on earth and things moved in heaven. He became such a heavenly being that it was not possible for him to stay here any longer. Oh, hallelujah! I believe God wants to bring all of us into line with His will, so that we shall penetrate into the heavenlies and become so empowered that we shall see signs and wonders and divers gifts of the Holy Spirit in our midst. These are wonderful days—these days of the outpouring of the Holy Spirit. You ask me, "When would you have liked to come to earth?" My answer is, "Just now. It suits me beautifully to know that I can be filled with the Holy Spirit, that I can be a temple in which He dwells, and that through this temple there shall be a manifestation of the power of God that will bring glory to His name."

Enoch conversed with God. I want to live in constant conversation with God. I am so grateful that from my youth up, God has given me a relish for the Bible. I find the Bible food for my soul. It is strength to the believer. It builds up our character in God. And as we receive with meekness the Word of God, we are being changed by the Spirit from glory to glory. And by this Book comes faith for faith cometh by hearing, and hearing by the Word of God (Rom. 10:17). And we know that "...without faith it is impossible to please him... (Heb. 11:6)."

I believe that all our failures come because of an imperfect understanding of God's Word. I see that it is impossible to please God on any other line but by faith, and everything that is not of faith is sin. You say, "How can I obtain this faith?" You see the secret in Hebrews 12:2, "Looking unto Jesus the author and finisher of our faith...." He is the author of faith. Oh, the might of our Christ who created the universe and upholds it all by the might of His power! God has chosen Him and ordained Him and clothed Him, and He who made this vast universe will make us a new creation. He spoke the Word and the stars came into being, can He not speak the Word that will produce a mighty faith in us? Ah, this One who is the author and finisher of our faith comes and dwells within us, quickens us by His Spirit, and molds us by His will. He comes to live His life of faith within us and to be to us all that we need. And He who has begun a good work within us will complete it and perfect it; for He not only is the author but the finisher and perfecter of our faith.

...the word of God is quick, and powerful, and sharper than any twoedged sword, piercing even to the dividing asunder of soul and

spirit, and of the joints and marrow, and is a discerner of the thoughts and intents of the heart.

Hebrews 4:12

How the Word of God severs the soul and the spirit—the soul which has a lot of carnality, a lot of selfishness in it, a lot of evil in it! Thank God, the Lord can sever from us all that is earthly and sensual, and make us a spiritual people. He can bring all our selfishness to the place of death, and bring the life of Jesus into our being to take the place of that earthly and sensual thing that is destroyed by the living Word.

The living Word pierces right to the very marrow. When I was in Australia, so many people came to me with double curvature of the spine; but the Word of the Lord came right down to the very marrow of their spines, and instantly they were healed and made straight, as I laid hands on them in the name of Jesus. The divine son of God, the living Word, through His power, moved upon those curvatures of the spine and straightened them out. Oh, thank God for the mighty power of the Word!

The Word of God comes in to separate us from everything that is not of God. It destroys. It also gives life. He must bring to death all that is carnal in us. It was after the death of Christ that God raised Him up on high, and as we are dead with Him we are raised up and made to sit in heavenly places in the new life that the Spirit gives.

God has come to lead us out of ourselves into Himself, and to take us from the ordinary into the extraordinary, from the human into the divine, and make us after the image of His Son. Oh, what a Savior! What an ideal Savior! It is written,

...now are we the sons of God, and it doth not yet appear what we shall be: but we know that, when he shall appear, we shall be like him; for we shall see him as he is.

1 John 3:2

But even now, the Lord wants to transform us from glory to glory, by the Spirit of the living God. Have faith in God, have faith in the Son, have faith in the Holy Spirit; and the triune God will work in you, working in you to will and to do all the good pleasure of His will.

Published in *The Pentecostal Evangel*

THE WORKING
OF MIRACLES

*There is healing through the blood of
Christ and deliverance for every captive.
God never intended His children to live in
misery because of some affliction that
comes directly from the devil.*

*Praying for a lady at Angeles Temple, Aimee Semple
McPherson's church in Los Angeles*

INSTRUCTIONS
FOR THE SICK
November 11, 1922

Is any sick among you? let him call for the elders of the church; and let them pray over him, anointing him with oil in the name of the Lord: And the prayer of faith shall save the sick, and the Lord shall raise him up; and if he hath committed sins, they shall be forgiven him.

James 5:14,15

We have in this precious word a real basis for the truth of healing. In this scripture God gives very definite instructions to the sick. If you are sick, your part is to call for the elders of the church; it is their part to anoint and pray for you in faith, and then the whole situation rests with the Lord. When you have been anointed and prayed for, you can rest assured that the Lord will raise you up. It is the Word of God.

I believe that we all can see that the church cannot play with this business. If any turn away from these clear instructions they are in a place of tremendous danger. Those who refuse to obey do so to their unspeakable loss.

James tells us in connection with this, "...if any of you do err from the truth, and one convert him; let him know, that he which converteth

the sinner from the error of his way shall save a soul from death..."
(James 5:19,20). Many turn away from the Lord like King Asa, who
sought the physicians in his sickness and consequently died, and I take it
that this passage means that if one induces another to turn back to the
Lord, he will save such from death and God will forgive a multitude of
sins that they have committed. This scripture can also have a large application on the line of salvation. If you turn away from any part of God's
truth, the enemy will certainly get an advantage over you.

Does the Lord meet those who look to Him for healing and obey
the instructions set forth in James? Most assuredly. Let me tell you a
story to show how He will undertake for the most extreme case.

One day I had been visiting the sick, and was with a friend of mine,
an architect, when I saw a young man from his office coming down the
road in a car holding in his hand a telegram. It contained a very urgent
request that we go immediately and pray for a man who was dying. We
went off in an auto as fast as possible and in about an hour and a half
reached a large house in the country where the man who was dying
resided. There were two staircases in that house, and it was extremely
convenient, for the doctors could go up and down one, and my friend
and I could go up and down the other, and so we had no occasion to
meet one another.

I found on arrival that it was a case of this sort. The man's body had
been broken, he was ruptured, and his bowels had been punctured in two
places. The discharge from the bowels had formed abscesses and blood
poisoning had set in. The man's face had turned green. Two doctors were
in attendance, but they saw that the case was beyond their power. They
had telegraphed to London for a great specialist, and, when we arrived,
they were at the railway station awaiting his arrival.

The man was very near death and could not speak. I said to his
wife, "If you desire, we will anoint and pray for him." She said, "That is
why I sent for you." I anointed him in the name of the Lord and asked
the Lord to raise him up. Apparently there was no change. God often
hides what He does. From day to day we find that God is doing wonderful things, and we receive reports of healings that have taken place that
we heard nothing about at the time of our meetings. Only last night a
woman came into the meeting suffering terribly. Her whole arm was

filled with poison, and her blood was so poisoned that it was certain to bring her to her death. We rebuked the thing, and she was here this morning and told us that she was without pain and had slept all night, a thing she had not done for two months. To God be all the praise. You will find He will do this kind of thing all along.

As soon as we anointed and prayed for this brother we went down the back staircase and the three doctors came up the front staircase. As we arrived downstairs, I said to my friend who had come with me, "Friend, let me have hold of your hands." We held each other's hands, and I said to him, "Look into my face and let us agree together according to Matthew 18:19 that this man should be brought out of this death." We laid the whole matter before God, and said, "Father, we believe."

Then the conflict began. The wife came down to us and said, "The doctors have got all their instruments out and they are about to operate." I cried, "What? Look here, he's your husband, and I tell you this, if those men operate on him, he will die. Go back and tell them you cannot allow it." She went back to the doctors and said, "Give me ten minutes." They said, "We can't afford to, the man is dying and it is your husband's only chance." She said, "I want ten minutes, and you don't touch his body until I have had them."

They went downstairs by one staircase and we went up by the other. I said to the woman, "This man is your husband, and he cannot speak for himself. It is now the time for you to put your whole trust in God and prove Him wholly true. You can save him from a thousand doctors. You must stand with God and for God in this critical hour." After that, we came down and the doctors went up. The wife faced those three doctors and said, "You shan't touch this man's body. He is my husband. I am sure that if you operate on him he will die, but he will live if you don't touch him."

Suddenly the man in the bed spoke. "God has done it," he said. They rolled back the bed clothes and the doctors examined him, and the abscesses were cut clear away. The nurse cleaned the place where they had been. The doctors could see the bowels still open and they said to the wife, "We know that you have great faith, and we can see that a miracle has taken place. But you must let us unite these broken parts and put in silver tubes, and we know that your husband will be all right after that, and it need not interfere with your faith at all." She said to them, "God has done the first thing and He can do the rest. No man shall touch him now." And God healed the whole thing. And that man is well and strong today. I can give his name and address to any who want it.

Do you ask by what power this was done? I would answer in the words of Peter, "...his name through faith in his name hath made this man strong..." (Acts 3:16). The anointing was done in the name of the Lord. And it is written, "The Lord shall raise him up." And He provides the double cure; even if sin has been the cause of the sickness, His Word declares, "If he have committed sins, they shall be forgiven."

You ask, "What is faith?" Faith is the principle of the Word of God. The Holy Spirit, who inspired the Word, is called the Spirit of Truth, and, as we receive with meekness the engrafted Word, faith springs up in our heart—faith in the sacrifice of Calvary; faith in the shed blood of Jesus; faith in the fact that He took our weakness upon Himself, has borne our sicknesses and carried our pains, and that He is our life today.

God has chosen us to help one another. We dare not be independent. He brings us to a place where we submit ourselves to one another. If we refuse to do this, we get away from the Word of God and out of the place of faith. I have been in this place once and I trust I shall never be there again. I went one time to a meeting. I was very, very sick, and I got worse and worse. I knew the perfect will of God was for me to humble myself and ask the elders to pray for me. I put it off and the meeting finished. I went home without being anointed and prayed with, and everyone in the house caught the thing I was suffering with.

My boys did not know anything else but to trust the Lord as the family Physician, and my youngest boy, George, cried out from the attic, "Dadda, come." I cried, "I cannot come. The whole thing is from me. I shall have to repent and ask the Lord to forgive me." I made up my mind to humble myself before the whole church. Then I rushed to the attic and laid my hands on my boy in the name of Jesus. I placed my hands on his head and the pain left and went lower down; he cried again, "Put your hands still lower." At last the pain went right down to the feet and as I placed my hand on the feet he was completely delivered. Some evil power had evidently gotten hold and as I laid my hands on the different parts of the body it left. (We have to see the difference between anointing the sick and casting out demons.) God will always be gracious when we humble ourselves before Him and come to a place of brokenness of spirit.

I was at a place one time ministering to a sick woman, and she said, "I'm very sick. I become all right for an hour, and then I have another attack." I saw that it was an evil power that was attacking her, and I learned something in that hour that I had never learned before. As I moved my hand down her body in the name of the Lord that evil power seemed to move just ahead of my hands and as I moved them down further and further the evil power went right out of her body and never returned.

I was in Havre in France and the power of God was being mightily manifested. A Greek named Felix attended the meeting and become very zealous for God. He was very anxious to get all the Catholics he could to the meeting in order that they should see that God was graciously visiting France. He found a certain bedridden woman who was fixed in a certain position and could not move, and he told her about the Lord healing at the meetings and that he would get me to come if she wished. She said, "My husband is a Catholic and he would never allow anyone who was not a Catholic to see me."

She asked her husband to allow me to come and told him what Felix had told her about the power of God working in our midst. He said, "I will have no Protestant enter my house." She said, "You know that the doctors cannot help me, and the priests cannot help, won't you let this man of God pray for me?" He finally consented and I went to the house. The simplicity of this woman and her childlike faith was beautiful to see.

I showed her my oil bottle and said to her, "Here is oil. It is a symbol of the Holy Ghost. When that comes upon you, the Holy Ghost will begin to work, and the Lord will raise you up." And God did something the moment the oil fell upon her. I looked toward the window and I saw Jesus. (I have seen Him often. There is no painting that is a bit like Him; no artist can ever depict the beauty of my lovely Lord.) The woman felt the power of God in her body and cried, "I'm free, my hands are free, my shoulders are free, and oh, I see Jesus! I'm free! I'm free!"

The vision vanished and the woman sat up in bed. Her legs were still bound, and I said to her, "I'll put my hands over your legs and you will be free entirely." And as I put my hands on those legs covered with bed clothes, I looked and saw the Lord again. She saw Him too and cried, "He's there again. I'm free! I'm free!" She rose from her bed and walked round the room praising God, and we were all in tears as we saw His wonderful works. The Lord shall raise them up when conditions are met.

When I was a young man I always loved the fellowship of old men, and was always careful to hear what they had to say. I had a friend, an old Baptist minister who was a wonderful preacher. I spent much of my time with him. One day he came to me and said, "My wife is dying." I said, "Brother Clark, why don't you believe God? God can raise her up if you will only believe Him." He asked me to come to his house, and I looked for someone to go with me.

I went to a certain rich man who was very zealous for God, and spent much money in opening up rescue missions, and I asked him to go with me. He said, "Never you mind me. You go yourself, but I don't take to this kind of business." Then I thought of a man who could pray by the hour. When he was on his knees he could go round the world three times and come out at the same place. I asked him to go with me and said to him, "You'll have a real chance this time. Keep at it, and quit when you're through." (Some go on longer after they are through.)

Brother Nichols, for that was his name, went with me and started praying. He asked the Lord to comfort the husband in his great bereavement and prayed for the orphans and a lot more on this line. I cried, "Oh, my God, stop this man." But there was no stopping him and he went on praying and there was not a particle of faith in anything he uttered. He did stop at last, and I said, "Brother Clark, it's now your turn to pray." He started, "Lord, answer the prayer of my brother and comfort me in this great bereavement and sorrow. Prepare me to face this great trial." I cried out, "My God, stop this man." The whole atmosphere was being charged with unbelief.

I had a glass bottle full of oil and I went up to the woman and poured the whole lot on her in the name of Jesus. Suddenly Jesus appeared, standing at the foot of the bed. He smiled and vanished. The woman stood up, perfectly healed, and she is a strong woman today.

We have a big God. We have a wonderful Jesus. We have a glorious Comforter. God's canopy is over you and will cover you at all times, preserving you from evil. Under His wings shalt thou trust. The Word of God is living and powerful and in its treasures you will find eternal life. If you dare trust this wonderful Lord, the Lord of life, you will find in Him everything you need.

So many are tampering with drugs, quacks, pills and plasters. Clear them all out and believe God. It is sufficient to believe God. You will find that if you dare trust Him, He will never fail. "The prayer of faith shall save the sick, and the Lord shall raise him up." Do you trust Him? He is worthy to be trusted.

I was one time asked to go to Weston-super-mare, a seaside resort in the West of England. I learned from a telegram that a man had lost his reason and had become a raving maniac, and they wanted me to go to pray for him. I arrived at the place, and the wife said to me, "Will you sleep with my husband?" I agreed, and in the middle of the night an evil power laid hold of him. It was awful. I put my hand on his head and his hair was like a lot of sticks. God gave deliverance—a temporary deliverance. At 6 o'clock the next morning, I felt that it was necessary that I should get out of that house for a short time.

The man saw me going and cried out, "If you leave me, there is no hope." But I felt that I had to go. As I went out I saw a woman with a Salvation Army bonnet on and I knew that she was going to their 7 o'clock prayer meeting. I said to the Captain who was in charge of the meeting, when I saw he was about to give out a hymn, "Captain, don't sing. Let's get to prayer." He agreed, and I prayed my heart out, and then I grabbed my hat and rushed out of the hall. They all thought they had a madman in their prayer meeting that morning.

I went down to the end of the parade, and there was the man I had spent the night with, rushing down toward the sea, without a particle of clothing on, about to drown himself. I cried, "In the name of Jesus, come out of him." The man fell full length on the ground and that evil power went out of him never to return. His wife came rushing after him, and the husband was restored to her in a perfect mental condition.

There are evil powers, but Jesus is greater than all evil powers. There are tremendous diseases, but Jesus is healer. There is no case too hard for Him. The Lion of Judah shall break every chain. He came to relieve the oppressed and to set the captive free. He came to bring redemption, to make us as perfect as man was before the fall.

People want to know how to be kept by the power of God. Every position of grace into which you are led—forgiveness, healing, deliverance of any kind—will be contested by satan. He will contend for your body. When you are saved, satan will come round and say, "See, you are not saved." The devil is a liar. If he says you are not saved, it is a sure sign that you are.

You will remember the story of the man who was swept and garnished. The evil power had been swept out of him. But the man remained in a stationary position. If the Lord heals you, you dare not remain in a stationary position. The evil spirit came back to that man and found the house swept, and took seven others worse than himself, and the last stage of that man was worse than the first. Be sure and get filled with God. Get an Occupier. Be filled with the Spirit.

God has a million ways of undertaking for those who go to Him for help. He has deliverance for every captive. He loves you so much that He even says, "Before they call, I will answer." Don't turn Him away.

Published in *The Pentecostal Evangel*

HEALING AND MIRACLES—
THE WAY OF GOD
August 4, 1923

God has given us much in these last days, and where much is given much will be required. The Lord has said to us,

Ye are the salt of the earth: but if the salt have lost his savour, wherewith shall it be salted? it is thenceforth good for nothing, but to be cast out, and to be trodden under foot of men.

Matthew 5:13

We see a thought on the same line when our Lord Jesus says,

If a man abide not in me, he is cast forth as a branch, and is withered; and men gather them, and cast them into the fire, and they are burned.

John 15:6

On the other hand He tells us,

If ye abide in me, and my words abide in you, ye shall ask what ye will, and it shall be done unto you.

John 15:7

If we do not move on with the Lord these days, and do not walk in the light of revealed truth, we shall become as the savorless salt, as a withered branch. This one thing we must do, forgetting those things that are behind, the past failures and the past blessings, we must reach forth for those things which are before, and press toward the mark for the prize of our high calling of God in Christ Jesus (Phil. 3:13,14).

For many years the Lord has been moving me on and keeping me from spiritual stagnation. When I was in the Wesleyan Methodist Church I was sure I was saved and was sure I was all right. The Lord said to me, "Come out," and I came out. When I was with the people known as the Brethren I was sure I was all right now. But the Lord said, "Come out." Then I went into the Salvation Army. At that time it was full of life and there were revivals everywhere. But the Salvation Army went into natural things and the great revivals that they had in those early days ceased. The Lord said to me, "Come out," and I came out. I have had to come out three times since. I believe that this Pentecostal revival that we are now in is the best thing that the Lord has on the earth today, and yet I believe that God has something out of this that is going to be still better. God has no use for any man who is not hungering and thirsting for yet more of Himself and His righteousness.

The Lord has told us to covet earnestly the best gifts, and we need to be covetous for those that will bring Him most glory. We need to see the gifts of healing and the working of miracles in operation today. Some say that it is necessary for us to have the gift of discernment in operation with the gifts of healing, but even apart from this gift I believe the Holy Ghost will have a divine revelation for us as we deal with the sick. Most people seem to have discernment, or think they have, and if they would turn it on themselves for twelve months they would never want to discern again. The gift of discernment is not criticism. I am satisfied that in Pentecostal circles today that our paramount need is more perfect love.

Perfect love will never want the preeminence in everything, it will never want to take the place of another, it will always be willing to take the back seat. If you go to a convention there is always someone who wants to give a message, who wants to be heard. If you have a desire to go to a convention you should have three things settled in your mind. Do I want to be heard? Do I want to be seen? Do I want anything on the line of finances? If I have these things in my heart, I have no right to be there. The one thing that must move us must be the constraining love of God to minister for Him. A preacher always loses out when he gets his mind on finances. It is well for Pentecostal preachers to avoid making much of finances except to stir up people to help our missionaries on financial lines. A preacher who gets big collections for the missionaries need never fear, the Lord will take care of his finances. A preacher should not land at a place and say that God had sent him. I am always fearful when I hear a man advertising this. If he is sent of God, the saints will know it. God has His plans for His servants and we must so live in His plans that He will place us where He wants us. If you seek nothing but the will of God, He will always put you in the right place at the right time. I want you to see that the gifts of healing and the working of miracles are part of the Spirit's plan and will come forth in operation as we are working along that plan. I must know the movement of the Spirit, and the voice of God. I must understand the will of God if I am to see the gifts of the Spirit in operation.

The gifts of healing are so varied. You may go and see ten people and every case is different. I am never happier in the Lord than when I am in a bedroom with a sick person. I have had more revelations of the Lord's presence when I have ministered to the sick at their bedsides than at any other time. It is as your heart goes out to the needy ones in deep compassion that the Lord manifests His presence. You are able to locate their position. It is then that you know that you must be filled with the Spirit to deal with the conditions before you.

Where people are in sickness you find frequently that they are dense about Scripture. They usually know three scriptures though. They know about Paul's thorn in the flesh, and that Paul told Timothy to take a little wine for his stomach's sake, and that Paul left someone sick somewhere; they forget his name, and don't remember the name of the place, and don't know where the chapter is. Most people think they have a thorn in the flesh. The chief thing in dealing with a person who is sick is to locate their exact position. As you are ministering under the Spirit's power, the Lord will let you see just that which will be the most helpful and the most faith-inspiring to them.

When I was in the plumbing business I enjoyed praying for the sick. Urgent calls would come and I would have no time to wash, and with my hands all black I would preach to these sick ones, my heart all aglow with love. Ah, you must have your heart in the thing when you pray for the sick. You have to get right to the bottom of the cancer with a divine compassion and then you will see the gifts of the Spirit in operation.

I was called at 10 o'clock one night to pray for a young person given up by the doctor who was dying of consumption. As I looked, I saw that unless God undertook it was impossible for her to live. I turned to the mother and said, "Well, Mother, you will have to go to bed." She said, "Oh, I have not had my clothes off for three weeks." I said to the daughters, "You will have to go to bed," but they did not want to go. It was the same with the son. I put on my overcoat and said, "Good-bye, I'm off." They said, "Oh, don't leave us." I said, "I can do nothing here." They said, "Oh, if you will stop, we will all go to bed." I knew that God would move nothing in an atmosphere of mere natural sympathy and unbelief.

They all went to bed and I stayed, and that was surely a time as I knelt by that bed face to face with death and with the devil. But God can change the hardest situation and make you know that He is almighty.

Then the fight came. It seemed as though the heavens were brass. I prayed from 11:00 p.m. to 3:30 in the morning. I saw the glimmering light on the face of the sufferer and saw her pass away. The devil said, "Now you are done for. You have come from Bradford and the girl has died on your hands." I said, "It can't be. God did not send me here for nothing. This is a time to change strength." I remembered that passage which said, "...men ought always to pray, and not to faint" (Luke 18:1). Death had taken place but I knew that my God was all powerful, and He that had split the Red Sea is just the same today. It was a time when I would not have "No," and God said "Yes." I looked at the window and at that moment the face of Jesus appeared. It seemed as though a million rays of light were coming from His face. As He looked at the one who had just passed away, the color came back to the face. She rolled over and fell asleep. Then I had a glorious time. In the morning she woke early, put on a dressing gown, and walked to the piano. She started to play and to sing a wonderful song. The mother and the sister and the brother had all come down to listen. The Lord had undertaken. A miracle had been wrought.

The Lord is calling us along this way. I am thanking God for difficult cases. The Lord has called us into heart union with Himself; He
wants His bride to have one heart and one Spirit with Him and to do
what He Himself loved to do. That case had to be a miracle. The lungs
were gone, they were just in shreds, but the Lord restored lungs that
were perfectly sound.

There is a fruit of the Spirit that must accompany the gift of healing and that is longsuffering. The man who is going through with God to
be used in healing must be a man of longsuffering. He must be always
ready with a word of comfort. If the sick one is in distress and helpless
and does not see everything eye to eye with you, you must bear with
them. Our Lord Jesus Christ was filled with compassion and lived and
moved in a place of longsuffering, and we will have to get into this place
if we are to help needy ones.

There are some times when you pray for the sick and you are
apparently rough. But you are not dealing with a person. You are dealing
with satanic forces that are binding the person. Your heart is full of love
and compassion to all, but you are moved to a holy anger as you see the
place the devil has taken in the body of the sick one, and you deal with
his position with a real forcefulness. One day a pet dog followed a lady
out of her house and ran all round her feet. She said to the dog, "My
dear, I cannot have you with me today." The dog wagged its tail and made
a big fuss. She said, "Go home, my dear." But the dog did not go. At last
she shouted roughly, "Go home," and off it went. Some people deal with
the devil like that. The devil can stand all the comfort you like to give
him. Cast him out! You are dealing not with the person, you are dealing
with the devil. Demon power must be dislodged in the name of the
Lord. You are always right when you dare to deal with sickness as with
the devil. Much sickness is caused by some misconduct, there is something wrong, there is some neglect somewhere, and satan has had a
chance to get in. It is necessary to repent and confess where you have
given place to the devil, and then he can be dealt with.

When you deal with a cancer case, recognize that it is a living evil
spirit that is destroying the body. I had to pray for a woman in Los Angeles one time who was suffering with cancer, and as soon as it was cursed
it stopped bleeding. It was dead. The next thing that happened was that
the natural body pressed it out, because the natural body had no room

for dead matter. It came out like a great big ball with tens of thousands of fibers. All these fibers had been pressing into the flesh. These evil powers move to get further hold of the system, but the moment they are destroyed their hold is gone. Jesus said to His disciples that He gave them power to loose and power to bind. It is our privilege in the power of the Holy Ghost to loose the prisoners of satan and to let the oppressed go free.

Take your position in the First Epistle of John and declare, "...greater is he that is in [me], than he that is in the world" (1 John 4:4). Then recognize that it is not yourself that has to deal with the power of the devil, but the Greater One that is in you. Oh, what it means to be filled with Him. You can do nothing of yourself, but He that is in you will win the victory. Your being has become the temple of the Spirit. Your mouth, your mind, your whole being becomes exercised and worked upon by the Spirit of God.

I was called to a certain town in Norway. The hall seated about 1,500 people. When I got to the place it was packed, and hundreds were trying to get in. There were some policemen there. The first thing I did was to preach to the people outside the building. Then I said to the policemen, "It hurts me very much that there are more people outside than inside and I feel I must preach to the people. I would like you to get me the marketplace to preach in." They secured for me a great park and a big stand was erected and I was able to preach to thousands. After the preaching, we had some wonderful cases of healing. One man came 100 miles bringing his food with him. He had not been passing anything through his stomach for over a month as he had a great cancer on his stomach. He was healed at that meeting, and opening his parcel, he began eating before all the people. There was a young woman there with a stiff hand. Instead of the mother making the child use her arm, she had allowed the child to keep the arm dormant until it was stiff, and she had grown up to be a young woman and was like the woman that was bowed down with the spirit of infirmity. As she stood before me I cursed the spirit of infirmity in the name of Jesus. It was instantly cast out and the arm was free. Then she waved it all over. At the close of the meeting the devil laid out two people with fits. When the devil is manifesting himself, then is the time to deal with him. Both of these people were delivered, and when they stood up and thanked and praised the Lord, what a wonderful time we had.

We need to wake up and be on the stretch to believe God. Before God could bring me to this place, He has broken me 1,000 times. I have wept, I have groaned. I have travailed many a night until God broke me. It seems to me that until God has mowed you down you never can have this longsuffering for others. We can never have the gifts of healing and the working of miracles in operation only as we stand in the divine power that God gives us and we stand believing God, and having done all we still stand believing.

We have been seeing wonderful miracles these last days and they are only a little of what we are going to see. I believe that we are right on the threshold of wonderful things, but I want to emphasize that all these things will be through the power of the Holy Ghost. You must not think that these gifts will fall upon you like ripe cherries. There is a sense in which you have to pay the price for everything you get. We must be covetous for God's best gifts, and say Amen to any preparation the Lord takes us through, in order that we may be humble, useable vessels through whom He Himself can operate by means of the Spirit's power.

Published in *The Pentecostal Evangel*

Wigglesworth once said that he would give any man an English pound if he caught him without his New Testament that he carried with him at all times.

DIVINE LIFE BRINGS
DIVINE HEALTH
1925

Mark 1. See from this scripture how Jesus was quickened by the power of the Spirit of God, and how He was driven of the Spirit into the wilderness, and how John also was so filled with the Spirit of God that he had a "cry" within him, and the cry moved all Israel; showing that when God gets hold of a man in the Spirit he can have a new "cry"—something that should be in God's order.

BE FILLED WITH GOD

A man may cry for 50 years without the Spirit of the Lord, and the more he cries the less notice people would take of it; but if he were filled with the Holy Ghost and cried once, the people would feel the effects of it; so there is a necessity for every one of us to be filled with God. It is not sufficient to have just a "touch," or to be filled with a "desire." There is only one thing that will meet the needs of the people, and that is for you to be immersed in the life of God—God taking you, and making you so filled with His Spirit, till you live right in God; so that whether you eat or drink, or whatever you do, it may be all for the glory of God, and in that place you will find that all your strength and all your mind and all your soul are filled with a zeal, not only for worship, but for proclamation; proclamation accompanied by all the power of God, which must move satanic power, disturb the world, and make it feel upset.

The reason the world is not seeing Jesus is because Christian people are not filled with Jesus. They are satisfied with weekly meetings, and occasionally reading the Bible, and sometimes praying. Beloved, if God lays hold of you by the Spirit, you will find that there is an end of everything and a beginning of God, so that your whole body becomes seasoned with a divine likeness of God. He has begun not only to use you, but He has taken you in hand, so that you might be a vessel unto honor. And our lives are not to be for ourselves, for if we live unto ourselves we shall die; but if we, through the Spirit, do mortify the deeds of the body, we shall live. In this place we are subject to the powers of God; but he that liveth to himself shall die. The man in the former place lives a life of freedom and joy and blessing and service, and a life which brings blessing to others. God would have us see that we must live in the Spirit.

In this Scripture, we have two important factors in the Spirit. One is Jesus filled with the Holy Ghost, driven by the Spirit's power, and the other is John the Baptist, who was so filled with the Spirit of God that his one aim was to go out preaching. We find him in the wilderness. What a strange place to be in! Beloved, it was quite natural for Jesus after He had served a whole day amongst the multitudes to want to go to His Father and pray all night. Why? He wanted a source of strength and power, and an association with His Father which would bring everything else to a place of submission; and when Jesus came from the mountain after communion with His Father, and after being clothed with His Holy presence and Spirit, when He met the demon power it had to go out. When He met sickness, it had to leave. He came from the mountain with power to meet the needs of the people, whatever they were. I do not know what your state of grace is— whether you are saved or not; but it is an awful thing for me to see people, who profess to be Christian, lifeless and powerless, and in a place where their lives are so parallel with the world's that it is difficult to discriminate which place they are in, whether in the flesh or in the Spirit. Many people live in the place which is described to us by Paul in Romans 7:25:

...with the mind I myself serve the law of God; but with the flesh the law of sin.

That is the place where sin is in the ascendancy, but when the power of God comes to you, it is to separate you from yourself.

I want to talk till you are shaken and disturbed, and see where you are. If I can get you to search the Scriptures after I leave this place and see if I have been preaching according to the Word of God, then I shall be pleased. Wake up to see that the Scriptures have life for you—they have liberty and freedom, and nothing less than to make you sons of God, free in the Holy Ghost.

Now Jesus came to bring us back what was forfeited in the Garden. Adam and Eve were there—free from sin and disease and first sin came, then disease, and then death came after, and people want to say it is not so! But I tell you, "Get the devil out of you, and you will have a different body. Get disease out, and you will get the devil out."

Jesus rebuked sickness, and it went, and so this morning, I want to bring you to a place where you will see that you are healed. You must give God your life: you must see that sickness has to go and God has to come in; that your lives have to be clean, and God will keep you holy; that you have to walk before God, and He will make you perfect, for God says, "Without holiness no man shall see Him," and as we walk in the light, as He is in the light, we have fellowship one with another, and the blood of Jesus Christ, God's Son, cleanseth us from all sin.

From Bondage to Victory

I want to say to you believers that there is a very blessed place for you to attain to, and the place where God wants you is a place of victory. When the Spirit of the Lord comes into your life it must be victory. The disciples, before they received the Holy Ghost, were always in bondage. Jesus said to them one day, just before the crucifixion, "One of you shall betray Me," and they were so conscious of their inability and their human depravity and helplessness that they said one to another, "Is it I?" And then Peter was ashamed that he had taken that stand, and he rose up and said, "Though all men deny Thee, yet will not I." And likewise the others rose and declared that neither would they; but they—every one—did leave Him.

173

But, beloved, after they received the power of the inducement of the Holy Ghost upon them, if you remember, they were made like lions to meet any difficulty. They were made to stand any test, and these men that failed before the crucifixion, when the power of God fell upon them in the upper room, they came out in front of all those people who were gathered together and accused them of crucifying the Lord of glory. They were bold. What had made them so? I will tell you. Purity is bold. Take, for instance, a little child. It will gaze straight into your eyes for as long as you like, without winking once. The more pure, the more bold; and I tell you, God wants to bring us into that divine purity of heart and life—that holy boldness. Not officiousness; not swelled-headness; not self-righteousness; but a pure, holy, divine appointment by One Who will come in and live with you, defying the powers of satan, and standing you in a place of victory—overcoming the world.

You never inherited that from the flesh. That is a gift of God, by the Spirit, to all who obey. And so, none can say they wish they were over-comers, but that they have failed and failed until they have no hope. Brother, God can make you an overcomer. When the Spirit of God comes into your body He will transform you, He will quicken you. Oh, there is a life in the Spirit which makes you free from the law of sin and death, and there is an audacity about it—also, there is a personality about it. It is the personality of the Deity. It is God in you.

I tell you this morning that God is able to so transform and change and bring you into order by the Spirit that you can become a new creation after God's order. There is no such thing as defeat for the believer. Without the cross, without Christ's righteousness, without the new birth, without the indwelling Christ, without this divine incoming of God, I see myself a failure. But God, the Holy Ghost, can come in and take our place till we are renewed in righteousness—made the children of God. Nay, verily, the sons of God.

Do you think that God would make you to be a failure? God has never made man to be a failure. He made man to be a "son"; to walk about the earth in power; and so when I look at you I know that there is a capability that can be put into you which has the capacity of con-trolling and bringing everything into subjection. Yes, there is the capacity of the power of Christ to dwell in you, to bring every evil thing under you till you can put your feet upon it, and be master over the flesh and the devil; till within you nothing rises except that which will magnify and glorify the Lord; and this morning God wants me to show you these disciples, who were so frail, like you and me, that we, too, may now be filled with God, and become pioneers of this wonderful truth I am preaching. Here we see Peter frail, helpless, and, at every turn of the tide, a failure. And God filled that man with the Spirit of His righteousness, till he went up and down, bold as a lion, and when he came to death—even crucifixion—he counted himself unworthy of being crucified like his Lord, and asked that his murderers would put him head downward on the tree. There was a deep submissiveness, and a power that was greater than all flesh. Peter had changed into the power of God.

The Scriptures do not tell two stories. They tell the truth. I want you to know the truth, and the truth will set you free. What is truth? Jesus said, "I am the Way, the Truth, and the Life." "He that believeth on me, as the Scriptures have said, out of his innermost being shall flow forth rivers of living water." This He spake of the Spirit that should be given them after Jesus was glorified.

I do not find anything in the Bible but holiness, and nothing in the world but worldliness. Therefore, if I live in the world I shall become worldly; but, on the other hand, if I live in the Bible, I shall become holy. This is the truth, and the truth will set you free. The power of God can remodel you. He can make you hate sin and love righteousness. He can take away bitterness and hatred and covetousness and malice, and can so consecrate you by His power, through His blood, that you are made pure—every bit holy. Pure in mind, heart and actions—pure right through. God has given me the way of life, and I want to give it to you, as though this were the last day I had to live. Jesus is the best there is for you, and you can each take Him away with you this morning. God gave His Son to be the propitiation for your sins, and not only so, but also for the sins of the whole world.

Jesus came to make us free from sin—free from disease and pain. When I see a person diseased and in pain I have great compassion for them, and when I lay my hands upon them, I know God means men to be so filled with Him that the power of sin shall have no effect upon them, and they shall go forth, as I am doing, to help the needy, sick, and afflicted. But what is the main thing? To preach the Kingdom of God and His righteousness. Jesus came to do this. John came preaching repentance. The disciples began by preaching repentance toward God, and faith in the Lord Jesus Christ, and I tell you, beloved, if you have really been changed by God, there is a repentance in your heart never to be repented of.

Through the revelation of the Word of God we find that divine healing is solely for the glory of God, and salvation is to make you know that now you have to be inhabited by another, even God, and you have to walk with God in newness of life.

Originally published by *Victory Press*
North Melbourne, Australia

JESUS CAN HEAL YOU, JESUS WANTS TO HEAL YOU

October 1924

Matthew 8:1-17. Here we have a wonderful word. All the Word is wonderful. This blessed Book brings such life and health and peace, and in such an abundance that we should never be poor anymore. This Book is my heavenly bank. I find everything I want in it. I want to show you how rich you may be, that in everything you can be enriched in Christ Jesus. He has abundance of grace for you and the gift of righteousness, and through His abundant grace all things are possible. I want to show you that you can be a living branch of the living Vine, Christ Jesus, and that it is your privilege to be right here in this world what He is. John tells us, "…as he is, so are we in this world" (1 John 4:17). Not that we are anything in ourselves, but Christ within us is our all in all.

The Lord Jesus is always wanting to show forth His grace and love in order to draw us to Himself. God is willing to do things, to manifest His Word, and let us know in measure the mind of our God in this day and hour. There are many needy ones, many afflicted ones, but I do not think any present are half as bad as this first case that we read of in Matthew 8. This man was a leper. You may be suffering with consumption or cancers or other things, but God will show forth His perfect cleansing, His perfect healing, if you have a living faith in Christ. He is a wonderful Jesus.

This leper must have been told about Jesus. How much is missed because people are not constantly telling what Jesus will do in this our day. Probably someone had come to that leper and said, "Jesus can heal you." And so he was filled with expectation as he saw the Lord coming down the mountainside. Lepers were not allowed to come within reach of people, they were shut out as unclean. And so in the ordinary way it would have been very difficult for him to get near because of the crowd that surrounded Jesus. But as He came down from the mount, He met, He came to the leper. Oh, this terrible disease! There was no help for him humanly speaking, but nothing is too hard for Jesus. The man cried, "...Lord, if thou wilt, thou canst make me clean" (Matt. 8:2). Was Jesus willing? You will never find Jesus missing an opportunity of doing good. You will find that He is always more willing to work than we are to give Him an opportunity to work. The trouble is, we do not come to Him, we do not ask Him for what He is more than willing to give.

And Jesus put forth His hand, and touched him, saying, "...I will; be thou clean. And immediately his leprosy was cleansed" (Matt. 8:3). I like that. If you are definite with Him, you will never go away disappointed. The divine life will flow into you and instantaneously you will be delivered. This Jesus is just the same today, and He says to you, "I will; be thou clean." He has an overflowing cup for thee, a fullness of life. He will meet you in your absolute helplessness. All things are possible if you will only believe. God has a real plan. It is so simple. Just come to Jesus. You will find Him just the same as He was in days of old.

The next case we have in this chapter is that of the centurion coming and beseeching Jesus on behalf of his servant who was sick of the palsy and grievously tormented. This man was so in earnest that he came seeking for Jesus. Notice this, that there is one thing certain, there is no such thing as seeking without finding. He that seeketh findeth. Listen to the gracious words of Jesus, "...I will come and heal him" (Matt. 8:7). Most places that we go to, there are so many people that we cannot pray for. In some places there are 200 or 300 who would like us to visit them, but we are not able to do so. But I am so glad that the Lord Jesus is always willing to come and heal. He longs to meet the sick ones. He loves to heal them of their afflictions. The Lord is healing many people today by means of handkerchiefs as you read that He healed people in the days of Paul. You can read of this in Acts 19:12.

A woman came to me in the city of Liverpool and said, "I would like you to help me. I wish you would join me in prayer. My husband is a drunkard and every night comes into the home under the influence of drink. Won't you join me in prayer for him?" I said to the woman, "Have you a handkerchief?" She took out a handkerchief and I prayed over it and told her to lay it on the pillow of the drunken man. He came home that night and laid his head on the pillow in which this handkerchief was tucked. He laid his head on more than the pillow that night. He laid his head on the promise of God. In Mark 11:24, we read:

> ...*What things soever ye desire, when ye pray, believe that ye receive them, and ye shall have them.*

The next morning the man got up and called at the first saloon that he had to pass on his way to work and ordered some beer. He tasted it and said to the bartender, "You have put some poison in this beer." He could not drink it, and went on to the next saloon and ordered some more beer. He tasted it and said to the man behind the counter, "You put some poison in this beer; I believe you folks have agreed to poison me." The bartender was indignant at being thus charged. The man said, "I will go somewhere else." He went to another saloon and the same thing happened as in the two previous saloons. He made such a fuss that they turned him out. After he came out from work he went to another saloon to get some beer, and again he thought he had been poisoned and he made such a disturbance that he was thrown out. He went to his home and told his wife what had happened and said, "It seems as though all the fellows have agreed to poison me." His wife said to him, "Can't you see the hand of the Lord in this, that He is making you dislike the stuff that has been your ruin?" This word brought conviction to the man's heart and he came to the meeting and got saved. The Lord has still power to set the captives free.

Jesus was willing to go and heal the sick one, but the centurion said, "Lord, I am not worthy that thou shouldst come under my roof: but speak the word only, and my servant shall be healed" (Matt. 8:8). Jesus was delighted with this expression and said to the man, "...Go thy way;

and as thou hast believed, so be it done unto thee. And his servant was healed in the selfsame hour" (Matt. 8:13).

I received a telegram once urging me to visit a case about 200 miles from my home. As I went to this place I met the father and mother and found them brokenhearted. They led me up a staircase to a room, and I saw a young woman on the floor and five people were holding her down. She was a frail young woman, but the power in her was greater than all those young men. As I went into the room, the evil powers looked out of her eyes and they used her lips saying, "We are many, you can't cast us out." I said, "Jesus can." He is equal to every occasion. He is waiting for an opportunity to bless. He is ready for every opportunity to deliver souls. When we receive Jesus it is true of us, "...greater is he that is in you, than he that is in the world" (1 John 4:4). He is greater than all the powers of darkness. No man can meet the devil in his own strength, but any man filled with the knowledge of Jesus, filled with His presence, filled with His power, is more than a match for the powers of darkness. God has called us to be more than conquerors through Him that loved us.

The living Word is able to destroy satanic forces. There is power in the name of Jesus. I would that every window in the street had the name of Jesus written upon it. His name, through faith in His name, brought deliverance to this poor, bound soul, and 37 demons came out giving their names as they came forth. The dear woman was completely delivered and they were able to give her back her child. That night there was heaven in that home and the father and mother and son and his wife were all united in glorifying Christ for His infinite grace. The next morning we had a gracious time in the breaking of bread. All things are wonderful with our wonderful Jesus. If you would dare rest your all upon Him, things would take place and He would change the whole situation. In a moment, through the name of Jesus, a new order of things can be brought in.

In the world they are always having new diseases and the doctors cannot locate them. A doctor said to me, "The science of medicine is in its infancy, and really we doctors have no confidence in our medicine. We are always experimenting." But the man of God does not experiment. He knows, or ought to know, redemption in its fullness. He knows, or ought to know, the mightiness of the Lord Jesus Christ. He is not, or should not, be moved by outward observation, but should get divine revelation of the mightiness of the name of Jesus and the power of His blood. If we exercise our faith in the Lord Jesus Christ, He will come forth and get glory over all the powers of darkness.

> *When the even was come, they brought unto him many that were possessed with devils: and he cast out the spirits with his word, and healed all that were sick: That it might be fulfilled which was spoken by Esaias the prophet, saying, Himself took our infirmities, and bare our sicknesses.*
>
> *Matthew 8:16,17*

The work is done if you only believe it. It is done. Himself took our infirmities and bare our sickness. If you can only see the Lamb of God as He went to Calvary! He took our flesh that He might take upon Himself the full burden of all our sin and all the consequence of sin. There on the cross of Calvary the results of sin were also dealt with.

> *...as the children are partakers of flesh and blood, he also himself likewise took part of the same; that through death he might destroy him that had the power of death, that is, the devil; And deliver them who through fear of death were all their lifetime subject to bondage.*
>
> *Hebrews 2:14,15*

Through His death there is deliverance for you today.

Published in *Triumphs of Faith*

Smith Wigglesworth and his daughter, Alice

STORIES OF HEALING
May 1927

The healings at the meetings have been blessed. At every meeting the sick were invited to remain, but in many of the meetings Brother Wigglesworth would pray for all who would stand up and believe that the Lord would heal them. At other times he would ask any who had pain to stand up and he prayed for them from the platform.

A lady stood saying she had pain in her head, and gallstones causing suffering. When Brother Wigglesworth prayed, the power of the Spirit came upon her.

Healed of a tumor in hospital. Handkerchief taken from the evangelist and laid on the sick. Mrs. Ingram writes of a visit to a hospital, taking a handkerchief with her. Her friend was to be operated on on Monday. On Wednesday when she visited her, her friend told her that she had been on the operating table and the ether had been administered. When she came to herself she discovered they had not operated because they said there was no need now for the operation. She was able to get up and the swelling was all gone.

High blood pressure. Mrs. A. Lavery, of Collingwood writes, "I thank God for the blessed healing power. Hands were laid on my head; I had blood pressure pains in my head for one year and six months night and day. I know I am healed."

Displaced kidneys, running ear. Mrs. Green, 23 Hardy Street, East Brunswick, testifies, "I had mastoid trouble in my ear, and general weakness through my body, both of my kidneys have dropped an inch. I suffered terribly, but had relief when prayed for. My ear was discharging, now I am free."

Broken ribs, broken collar bone, pierced lungs. Mr. R. Eddison, 155 Hoddle Street, West Richmond, was injured in a car accident in 1926. He had his ribs broken, lungs pierced, and collar bone broken. He was in the hospital three weeks; had suffered much pain for three months, until prayed for in the meeting.

A woman who had been ill in bed sixteen weeks, was raised up by the Lord, baptized in water later, and the day following received the baptism of the Holy Spirit.

A dying baby was healed.

A woman who had suffered pain in her legs for eleven years was set free.

Mrs. Rose Jesule writes, "The Lord touched my body in the audience, and I am free."

Another writes, "I have received the second handkerchief which you prayed over, and the Lord is blessing. This cancer is slowly drying up. I have had no more hemorrhages and the terrible odor is leaving. Praise the Lord."

Meetings in Richmond Temple, Melbourne, Australia
Published in *Triumphs of Faith*

DO YOU WANT
TO BE HEALED?

September 1927

I believe the Word of God is so powerful that it can transform any and every life. There is power in God's Word to make that which does not appear to appear. There is executive power in the Word that proceeds from His lips. The psalmist tells us, "He sent His word, and healed them..." (Ps. 107:20). And do you think that Word has diminished in its power? I tell you nay, but God's Word can bring things to pass today as of old.

The psalmist said, "Before I was afflicted I went astray: but now have I kept thy word" (Ps. 119:67). And again, "It is good for me that I have been afflicted; that I might learn thy statutes" (Ps. 119:71). And if our afflictions will bring us to the place where we see that we cannot live by bread alone, but must partake of every word that proceedeth out of the mouth of God, they will have served a blessed purpose.

REST ASSURED

But I want you to realize that there is a life of purity, a life made clean through the Word He has spoken, in which, through faith, you can glorify God with a body that is free from sickness, as well as with a spirit set free from the bondage of satan.

Here they lay, a great multitude of impotent folk, of blind, halt, withered, around that pool, waiting for the moving of the water. Did Jesus heal everybody? He left many around that pool unhealed. There were doubtless many who had their eyes on the pool and who had no eyes for Jesus. There are many today who have their confidence all the time in things seen. If they would only get their eyes on God instead of on natural things, how quickly they would be helped.

The question arises: Is salvation and healing for all? It is for all who will press right in and get their portion. You remember the case of that Syrophenician woman who wanted the devil cast out of her daughter. Jesus said to her, "Let the children first be filled: for it is not meet to take the children's bread, and to cast it unto the dogs" (Mark 7:27). Note, healing and deliverance are here spoken of by the Master as "the children's bread;" so, if you are a child of God, you can surely press in for your portion.

The Syrophenician woman purposed to get from the Lord what she was after, and she said, "Yes, Lord: yet the dogs under the table eat of the children's crumbs" (Mark 7:28). Jesus was stirred as He saw the faith of this woman, and He told her, "For this saying go thy way; the devil is gone out of thy daughter" (Mark 7:29). Today there are many children of God refusing their blood-purchased portion of health in Christ and are throwing it away, while sinners are pressing through and picking it up from under the table, as it were, and are finding the cure not only for their bodies, but for their spirits and souls as well. The Syrophenician woman went home and found that the devil had indeed gone out of her daughter. Today there is bread, there is life, there is health for every child of God through His all-powerful Word.

> *Is any sick among you? let him call for the elders of the church; and let them pray over him, anointing him with oil in the name of the Lord: And the prayer of faith shall save the sick, and the Lord shall raise him up; and if he have committed sins, they shall be forgiven him.*
>
> *James 5:14,15*

We have in this precious Word a real basis for the truth of healing. In this scripture God gives very definite instructions to the sick. If you are sick, your part is to call for the elders of the church; it is their part to anoint and pray for you in faith, and then the whole situation rests with the Lord. When you have been anointed and prayed for, you can rest assured that the Lord will raise you up. It is the Word of God.

I believe that we all can see that the church cannot play with this business. If any turn away from these clear instructions they are in a place of tremendous danger. Those who refuse to obey, do so to their unspeakable loss.

James tells us in connection with this,

> *...if any of you do err from the truth, and one convert him; Let him know, that he which converteth the sinner from the error of his way shall save a soul from death....*
>
> *James 5:19,20*

Many turn away from the Lord, as did King Asa, who sought the physicians in his sickness and consequently died; and I take it that this passage means that if one induces another to turn back to the Lord, he will save such from death and God will forgive a multitude of sins that they have committed. This scripture can also have a large application on the line of salvation. If you turn away from any part of God's truth, the enemy will certainly get an advantage over you.

Does the Lord meet those who look to Him for healing and obey the instructions set forth in James? Most assuredly. Let me tell you a story to show how He will undertake for the most extreme case.

The Word can drive every disease away from you body. It is your portion in Christ who Himself is our bread, our life, our health, our all in all. And though you may be deep in sin, you can come to Him in repentance, and He will forgive and cleanse and heal you. His words are spirit and life to those who will receive them. There is a promise in the last verse in Joel, "...I will cleanse their blood that I have not cleansed..." (Joel 3:21). This is as much as to say He will provide new life within. The life of Jesus Christ, God's Son, can so purify men's hearts and minds that they become entirely transformed, spirit, soul, and body.

WILT THOU BE MADE WHOLE?

There they are round the pool; and this man had been there a long time. His infirmity was of 38 years' standing. Now and again an opportunity would come, as the angel stirred the waters, but his heart would be made sick as he saw another step in and be healed before him. But one day Jesus was passing that way, and seeing him lying there in that sad condition, enquired, "Wilt thou be made whole?" Jesus said it, and His Word is from everlasting to everlasting. This is His Word to you, poor, tried, and tested one today. You may say, like this poor impotent man, "I have missed every opportunity up till now." Never mind about that—*Wilt thou be made whole?*

I visited a woman who had been suffering for many years. She was all twisted up with rheumatism and had been two years in bed. I said to her, "What makes you lie here?" She said, "I've come to the conclusion that I have a thorn in the flesh." I said, "To what wonderful degree of righteousness have you attained that you have to have a thorn in the flesh? Have you had such an abundance of divine revelations that there is danger of your being exalted above measure?" She said, "I believe it is the Lord who is causing me to suffer." I said, "You believe it is the Lord's will for you to suffer, and you are trying to get out of it as quickly as you can. There are doctor's bottles all over the place. Get out of your hiding place and confess that you are a sinner. If you'll get rid of your self-righteousness, God will do something for you. Drop the idea that you are so holy that God has got to afflict you. Sin is the cause of your sickness and not righteousness. Disease is not caused by righteousness, but by sin.

There is healing through the blood of Christ and deliverance for every captive. God never intended His children to live in misery because of some affliction that comes directly from the devil. A perfect atonement was made at Calvary. I believe that Jesus bore my sins, and I am free from them all. I am justified from all things if I dare believe. He Himself took our infirmities and bare our sicknesses; and if I dare believe, I can be healed.

See this poor, helpless man at the pool. "Wilt thou be made whole?" But there is a difficulty in the way. The man has one eye on the pool and one on Jesus. There are many people getting cross-eyed this way these days; they have one eye on the doctor and one on Jesus. If you will only look to Christ and put both your eyes on Him you can be made every whit whole, spirit, soul, and body. It is the Word of the living God that they who believe should be justified, made free from all things. And whom the Son sets free is free indeed.

You say, "Oh, if I only could believe!" He understands. Jesus knew he had been a long time in that case. He is full of compassion. He knows that kidney trouble, He knows those corns, He knows that neuralgia. There is nothing He does not know. He only wants a chance to show Himself merciful and gracious to you. But He wants to encourage you to believe Him. If thou canst only believe, thou canst be saved and healed.

Dare to believe that Jesus was wounded for your transgressions, was bruised for your iniquities, was chastised that you might have peace, and that by His stripes there is healing for you right here and now. You have failed because you have not believed Him. Cry out to Him even now, "Lord, I believe, help Thou mine unbelief."

TESTIMONIES

I was in Long Beach, California, one day, and with a friend, was passing a hotel. He told me of a doctor there who had a diseased leg; that he had been suffering from it for six years, and could not get out. We went up to his room and found four doctors there. I said, "Well, doctor, I see you have plenty on, I'll call again another day." I was passing another time, and the Spirit said, "Go join thyself to him." Poor doctor! He surely was in a bad condition. He said, "I have been like this for six years, and nothing human can help me." I said, "You need God Almighty." People are trying to patch up their lives; but you cannot do anything without God. I talked to him for awhile about the Lord, and then prayed for him. I cried, "Come out of him, in the name of Jesus." The doctor cried, "It's all gone!"

Oh, if we only knew Jesus! One touch of His mightiness meets the need of every crooked thing. The trouble is to get people to believe Him. The simplicity of this salvation is so wonderful. One touch of living faith in Him is all that is required, and wholeness is your portion.

I was in Long Beach about six weeks later, and the sick were coming for prayer. Among those filling up the aisle was the doctor. I said, "What is the trouble?" He said, "Diabetes, but it will be all right tonight. I know it will be all right." There is no such thing as the Lord not meeting your need. There are no "ifs" or "mays;" His promises are all "shalls." All things are possible to him who believeth. Oh, the name of Jesus! There is power in that name to meet every condition of human need.

At that meeting there was an old man helping his son to the altar. He said, "He has fits—many every day." Then there was a woman with a cancer. Oh, what sin has done! We read that, when God brought forth His people from Egypt, "...there was not one feeble person among their tribes" (Ps. 105:37). No disease! All healed by the power of God! I believe that God wants a people like that today.

I prayed for the sister who had the cancer and she said, "I know I'm free and that God has delivered me." Then they brought the boy with the fits, and I commanded the evil spirits to leave, in the name of Jesus. Then I prayed for the doctor. At the next night's meeting the house was full. I called out, "Now, doctor, what about the diabetes?" He said, "It has gone." Then I said to the old man, "What about your son?" He said, "He hasn't had any fits since." We have a God who answers prayer.

Jesus meant this man at the pool to be a testimony forever. When he had both eyes on Jesus, He said to him, "Do the impossible thing. Rise, take up thy bed, and walk." Jesus called on the man with the withered hand to do the impossible—to stretch forth his hand, the man did the impossible thing—he stretched out his hand, and it was made every whit whole. And so with this impotent man—he began to rise, and he found the power of God moving within. He wrapped up his bed and began to walk off. It was the Sabbath day, and there were some of those folks around who think much more of a day than they do of the Lord; and they began to make a fuss. When the power of God is in manifestation, a protest will always come from some hypocrites. Jesus knew all about what the man was going through, and met him again; and this time He said to him, "Behold, thou are made whole: sin no more, lest a worse thing come unto thee" (John 5:14).

There is a close relationship between sin and sickness. How many know that their sickness is a direct result of sin? I hope that no one will come to be prayed for who is living in sin. But if you will obey God and repent of your sin and quit it, God will meet you, and neither your sickness nor your sin will remain. "...the prayer of faith shall save the sick, and the Lord shall raise him up; and if he have committed sins, they shall be forgiven him" (James 5:15).

Faith is just the open door through which the Lord comes. Do not say, "I was healed by faith." Faith does not save. God saves through that open door. Healing comes the same way. You believe, and the virtue of Christ comes. Healing is for the glory of God. I am here because God healed me when I was dying; and I have been all round the world preaching this full redemption, doing all I can to bring glory to the wonderful name of Jesus, through whom I was healed.

"Sin no more, lest a worse thing come upon thee." The Lord told us in one place about an evil spirit going out from a man. The house that he left got all swept and garnished, but it received no new occupant. And that evil spirit, with seven other spirits more wicked than himself, went back to that unoccupied house, and the last stage of the man was worse than the first.

The Lord does not heal you to go to a baseball game or a race meeting. He heals you for His glory and that from henceforth your life shall glorify Him. But this man remained stationary. He did not magnify God. He did not seek to be filled with the Spirit. And his last state became worse than the first.

The Lord would so cleanse the motives and desires of our hearts that we will seek but one thing only and that is, His glory. I went to a certain place one day and the Lord said, "This is for My glory." A young man had been sick for a long time confined to his bed in an utterly hopeless condition. He was fed only with a spoon, and was never dressed. The weather was damp, and so I said to the people of the house, "I wish you would put the young man's clothes by the fire to air." At first they would not take any notice of my request, but because I was persistent, they at last got out his clothes, and, when they were aired, I took them into his room.

The Lord said to me, "You will have nothing to do with this;" and I just lay out prostrate on the floor. The Lord showed me that He was going to shake the place with His glory. The very bed shook. I laid my hands on the young man in the name of Jesus, and the power fell in such a way that I fell with my face to the floor. In about a quarter of an hour the young man got up and walked up and down praising God. He dressed himself and then went out to the room where his father and mother were. He said, "God has healed me." Both the father and mother fell prostrate to the floor as the power of God surged through that room. There was a woman in that house who had been in an asylum for lunacy, and her condition was so bad that they were about to take her back. But the power of God healed her, too.

The power of God is just the same today as of old. Men need to be taken back to the old paths, to the old-time faith, to believe God's Word and every "thus saith the Lord" therein. The Spirit of the Lord is moving in these days. God is coming forth. If you want to be in the rising tide, you must accept all God has said.

"Wilt thou be made whole?" It is Jesus who says it. Give Him your answer. He will hear and He will answer.

Published in *The Bridal Call Foursquare*

PENTECOSTAL
MANIFESTATIONS
May 27, 1944

The motto of a cold, indifferent, worldly church is, "Respectability and decorum," respectability inspired by one who is far from respectable—satan.

The birth of the Church was announced by a rushing mighty wind, a tornado from heaven. Moffatt translates Acts 2:1, "During the course of Pentecost they were all together, when suddenly there came a sound from heaven like a violent blast of wind...." And all of the assembled company came under the power of that which was symbolized as a mighty tornado, a violent blast. Their whole beings were moved by it, so that onlookers thought they were full of new wine. The unnatural movement of their bodies was followed by a supernatural movement of their tongues, for they spoke in other tongues as the Spirit gave them utterance. Thus they received the enduement of power from on high.

The crowd saw the movements and heard the sounds. The sounds were comprehensible—some of them. The movements were incomprehensible—most of them. Some were amazed—those who could comprehend the languages—and the others were confounded. They could not understand the languages, but they thought they could understand the motions, and they interpreted them as the actions of drunken people. Some were amazed, others mocked—none understood.

A generation that prides itself upon its outer respectability and decorum despises the manifestations of the Spirit of God. Nevertheless it is written, "...the manifestation of the Spirit is given to every man to profit withal" (1 Cor. 12:7).

David danced or leaped before the ark of the Lord and he was considered vile by the daughter of the former king. The daughter of Saul accused the anointed of God of vileness in manifestation, want of respectability, of lack of decorum, before the ark of the Lord.

Did David stop when the wife of his bosom derided him? Did he acquiesce to the formalism she represented? He declared, "...I will yet be more vile than thus..." (2 Sam. 6:22). It was as if he had said, "If occasion requires it, I will leap higher and dance more."

There is great danger when some churches that have known the manifestation of the Spirit in days gone by desire to become so respectable and decorous that the supernatural is ruled out of their meetings. We need Peters today who can say in explanation of the Pentecostal phenomena in our midst, "...these are not drunken, as ye suppose...this is that..." (Acts 2:15,16). If we become so ultra-respectable and decorous that we rule out the supernatural, Peter will have nothing to apologize for. He will have to say, "This was that, but it is gone." We may as well write upon our assemblies, "Ichabod"—the glory has departed. We cease to be vile, and Michal will welcome us home.

There must be no compromise with Michals, with those who hate the supernatural, or they will draw us from the presence of the ark and cause us to cease to be joyful in the presence of the Lord. Michal would have been quite content to have the ark stay where it was.

Pentecost came with the sound of a mighty rushing wind, a violent blast from heaven! Heaven has not exhausted its blasts, but our danger is we are getting frightened of them. The apostles were not. They had a repetition. When they had been threatened to speak no more in the name of Jesus, they lifted up their voices to God in one accord, and prayed,

...behold their threatenings: and grant unto thy servants, that with all boldness they may speak thy word, By stretching forth thine hand to heal; and that signs and wonders may be done by the name of thy holy child Jesus.

Acts 4:29,30

And the place was shaken where they were assembled together, and all were filled afresh with the Holy Ghost. Pentecost repeated! Manifestation again! All filled—mouths and all! "And they spake the Word of God with"—what? hesitation, moderation, timidity? No, they were yet more vile. "They spake the Word of God with boldness." And the signs and wonders increased. They never resented the first manifestations on their body on the day of Pentecost, and they prayed and received the second experience—building and all. Even the place was shaken this time.

Our God is an active God. His thunder is just as loud today as it was in the first century. His lightning is just as vivid as it was in the days of the early church. The sound of the mighty rushing wind is just the same today as it was on the day of the Pentecost. Pray for the violent blasts of wind from heaven, expect them, and you will get them. And do not be afraid of them.

Let God deal with the Michals. David did not compromise. He was willing to have yet more manifestations of the Spirit. "I will yet be more vile." We can have Pentecost plus Pentecost, if we wish. God's arm is not shortened, nor is His ear heavy. He wants to show His hand and the strength of His arm today in convincing a gainsaying world by sight, sound, and instruction. Take note of Conybeare's translation of 1 Thessalonians 5:19, "Quench not the manifestation of the Spirit."

Published in *The Pentecostal Evangel*

ULTIMATE POWER

The Lord wants all saved people to receive power from on High—power to witness, power to act, power to live, and power to show forth the divine manifestation of God within.

Four generations of Wigglesworth: Grandfather, father, son, and grandson

STUNNED BY
THE POWER OF GOD
July 1915

I am convinced that there is nothing in the world that is going to convince men and women of the power of the Gospel like the manifestation of the Spirit with the fruits. God has baptized us in the Holy Ghost for a purpose, that He may show His mighty power in human flesh, as He did in Jesus, and He is bringing us to a place where He may manifest these gifts.

> *...no man speaking by the Spirit of God calleth Jesus accursed: and no man can say that Jesus is the Lord, but by the Holy Ghost.*
>
> *1 Corinthians 12:3*

Every man who does not speak the truth concerning this Word, which is Jesus, makes Him the accursed; so all we have to do is to have the revelation of the Word in our hearts and there will be no fear of our being led astray, because this Word is nothing else but Jesus. In the gospel of St. John you read that the Word was God, and He became flesh and dwelt amongst us and we beheld His glory, the glory of the only begotten Son of the Father. So it is revealed that He is the Son of God—the Word of God. This Word (pointing to the Bible) is nothing else than the Word of God, and everything that confesses it not you can put down straight away, without getting mixed up at all, that it is not of the Holy Ghost and consequently you can wipe out all such things. There is no difficulty about saving yourselves, because the Word of God will always save.

Now there are diversities of gifts, but the same Spirit. And there are diversities of administrations, but the same Lord. And there are diversities of operations, but it is the same God which worketh all in all. But the manifestation of the Spirit is given to every man to profit withal.

1 Corinthians 12:4-7

My heart is in this business. I am brought face to face with the fact that now the Holy Ghost is dwelling within me, that He is dwelling in my body, and as John says in his epistle, the unction of the Holy One is within. The unction of the Holy One is the Holy Spirit manifested in us. So we see that straight away within us there is the power to make manifest and bring forth those gifts which He has promised, and these gifts will be manifested in proportion as we live in the unction of the Spirit of God. Thus we shall find out that those gifts must be manifested.

My brother here (Mr. Moser) was suffering from want of sleep. He had had no full night of sleep for a long time. I said last night, "I command thee in the name of Jesus to sleep." When he came this morning he was well, he had had a good night's sleep. A man came to me in Toronto and said he had not had a night's rest for three years and that he had lost the power to sleep. He also said he had lost his business; what could we do for him? I said, "I command you in the name of the Lord Jesus to go home and sleep." Without questioning me further he went home, and at 8 o'clock the next morning he rung me up and said, "Can I see you? I want to see you soon. I have been sleeping at night." So he came, and then said, "Can you give me power to get my business back?" I said, "Come to the meeting tonight." He said, "I will." He came, and the power of the Lord filled the place. Conviction settled upon that man. A call was made to the altar. He came, but fell on the way. God saved him, and that was the turning point in his life and for his business. Beloved, the power of the Holy Ghost is within us to profit withal. He says,

To one is given by the Spirit the word of wisdom; to another the word of knowledge by the same Spirit; to another faith by the same Spirit; to another the gifts of healing by the same Spirit; to another the working of miracles; to another prophecy; to another discerning of spirits; to another divers kinds of tongues; to another the interpretation of tongues: But all these worketh that one and the selfsame Spirit, dividing to every man severally as he will.

1 Corinthians 12:8-11

Paul distinctly says that it is possible for any one man not to come behind in any gift according to the measure of faith as he receives of the Lord Jesus. No doubt some of you present have sometimes thought what a blessed thing it would be if you had been the Virgin Mary. Listen, "Blessed is the womb that bare thee, and the paps which thou hast sucked. But he said, Yea rather, blessed are they that hear the word of God, and keep it" (Luke 11:27,28). You see a higher position than Mary's is attained through simple faith in what the Scriptures say.

If we receive the Word of God as it is given to us, there will be power in our bodies to claim the gifts of God, and it will amaze the world when they see the power of God manifested through these gifts. I believe we are coming to a time when these gifts will be more distinctly manifested. What can be more convincing? Aye, He is a lovely Jesus. He went forth from place to place, rebuking demons, healing the sick, and doing other wonderful things. What was the reason? God was with Him.

Wherever there is a child of God who dare receive the Word of God and cherish it, there is God made manifest in the flesh, for the Word of God is life and spirit and brings us into a place where we know that we have power with God and with men, in proportion to our loyalty of faith in the Word of God.

Now, beloved, I feel somehow that we have missed the greatest principle which underlies the baptism of the Holy Spirit. The greatest principle is that God the Holy Ghost came into my body to make manifest the mighty works of God and that I may profit withal. Not one gift alone, but as God the Holy Ghost abides in my body I find He fills it, and then one can truly say it is the unction of the Holy One. It so fills us that we feel we can command demons to come out of persons possessed; and when I lay hands on the sick in the name of the Lord

Jesus I realize that this body is the outer coil merely and that within is the Son of God. For I receive the Word of Christ and Christ is in me, the power of God is in me, and the Holy Ghost is making that Word a living Word, and the Holy Ghost makes me say, "Come out!" It is not Wigglesworth. It is the power of the Holy Ghost that makes manifest the glorious presence of Christ.

Published in *Flames of Fire*

THE POWER OF THE NAME
January 20, 1923

Acts 3:1-16. All things are possible through the name of Jesus. "...God also hath highly exalted him, and given him a name which is above every name: that at the name of Jesus every knee should bow..." (Phil. 2:9,10). There is power to overcome everything in the world through the name of Jesus. I am looking forward to a wonderful union through the name of Jesus. There is none other name under heaven given among men whereby we must be saved.

I want to instill into you the power, the virtue, and the glory of that name. Six people went into the house of a sick man to pray for him. He was an Episcopalian vicar, and lay in his bed utterly helpless, without even strength to help himself. He had read a little tract about healing and had heard about people praying for the sick and sent for these friends, who, he thought, could pray the prayer of faith. He was anointed according to James 5:14, but, because he had no immediate manifestation of healing, he wept bitterly. The six people walked out of the room, somewhat crestfallen to see the man lying there in an unchanged condition.

When they were outside, one of the six said, "There is one thing we might have done. I wish you would all go back with me and try it." They went back and all got together in a group. This brother said, "Let us whisper the name of Jesus." At first when they whispered this worthy name, nothing seemed to happen. But as they continued to whisper, "Jesus! Jesus! Jesus!" the power began to fall. As they saw that God was beginning to work, their faith and joy increased and they whispered the name louder and louder. As they did so the man arose from his bed and dressed himself. The secret was just this, those six people had gotten their eyes off the sick man, and they were just taken up with the Lord Jesus Himself, and their faith grasped the power that there is in His name. Oh, if people would only appreciate the power that there is in this name, there is no telling what would happen.

I know that through His name and through the power of His name we have access to God. The very face of Jesus fills the whole place with glory. All over the world there are people magnifying that name, and oh, what a joy it is for me to utter it.

One day I went up into a mountain to pray. I had a wonderful day. It was one of the high mountains of Wales. I heard of one man going up this mountain to pray, and the Spirit of the Lord met him so wonderfully that his face shone like that of an angel when he returned. Everyone in the village was talking about it. As I went up to this mountain and spent the day in the presence of the Lord, His wonderful power seemed to envelope and saturate and fill me.

Two years before this time there had come to our house two lads from Wales. They were just ordinary lads but they became very zealous for God. They came to our mission and saw some of the works of God. They said to me, "We would not be surprised if the Lord brings you down to Wales to raise our Lazarus." They explained that the leader of their assembly was a man who had spent his days working in a tin mine and his nights preaching, and the result was that he collapsed, went into consumption, and for four years he had been a helpless invalid, having to be fed with a spoon.

When I was up on that mountaintop I was reminded of the transfiguration scene, and I felt that the Lord's only purpose in taking us into the glory was to fit us for greater usefulness in the valley.

TONGUES AND INTERPRETATION: "The living God has chosen us for His divine inheritance, and He it is who is preparing us for our ministry, that it may be of God and not of man."

As I was on the mountaintop that day, the Lord said to me, "I want you to go and raise Lazarus." I told the brother who accompanied me of this, and when we got down to the valley, I wrote a postcard: "When I was up on the mountain praying today, God told me that I was to go and raise Lazarus." I addressed the postcard to the man in the place whose name had been given to me by the two lads. When we arrived at the place we went to the man to whom I had addressed the card. He looked at me and said, "Did you send this?" I said, "Yes." He said, "Do you think we believe in this? Here, take it." And he threw it at me.

The man called a servant and said, "Take this man and show him Lazarus." Then he said to me, "The moment you see him you will be ready to go home. Nothing will hold you." Everything he said was true from the natural viewpoint. The man was helpless. He was nothing but a mass of bones with skin stretched over them. There was no life to be seen. Everything in him spoke of decay.

I said to him, "Will you shout? You remember that at Jericho the people shouted while the walls were still up. God has like victory for you if you will only believe." But I could not get him to believe. There was not an atom of faith there. He had made up his mind not to have anything.

It is a blessed thing to learn that God's Word can never fail. Never hearken to human plans. God can work mightily when you persist in believing Him in spite of discouragements from the human standpoint. When I got back to the man whom I had sent the postcard, he asked, "Are you ready to go now?" "I am not moved by what I see. I am moved only by what I believe. I know this. No man looks if he believes. No man feels if he believes. The man who believes God has it. Every man who comes into the Pentecostal condition can laugh at all things and believe God."

There is something in the Pentecostal work that is different from any-thing else in the world. Somehow in Pentecost you know that God is a real-ity. Wherever the Holy Ghost has right of way, the gifts of the Spirit will be in manifestation; and where these gifts are never in manifestation, I ques-tion whether He is present. Pentecostal people are spoiled for anything else than Pentecostal meetings. We want none of the entertainments that the churches are offering. When God comes in He entertains us Himself. Entertained by the King of kings and Lord of lords!! Oh, it is wonderful.

There were difficult conditions in that Welsh village, and it seemed impossible to get the people to believe. "Ready to go home?" I was asked. But a man and a woman there asked us to come and stay with them. I said, "I want to know how many of you people can pray." No one wanted to pray. I asked if I could get seven people to pray with me for the poor man's deliverance. I said to the two people who were going to entertain us, "I will count on you two, and there is my friend and myself, and we need three others." I told the people that I trusted that some of them would awaken to their privilege and come in the morning and join us in prayer for the raising of Lazarus. It will never do to give way to human opinions. If God says a thing, you have to believe it.

I told the people that I would not eat anything that night. When I got to bed it seemed as if the devil tried to place on me everything that he had placed on that poor man in the bed. When I awoke I had a cough and all the weakness of a tubercular subject. I rolled out of bed on to the floor and cried out to God to deliver me from the power of the devil. I shouted loud enough to wake everybody in the house, but nobody was disturbed. God gave victory and I got back into bed again as free as ever I was in my life. At 5 o'clock the Lord awakened me and said to me, "Don't break bread until you break it round My table." At 6 o'clock He gave me these words, "And I will raise him up." I put my elbow into the fellow who was sleeping with me. He said "Ugh!" I put my elbow into him again and said, "Do you hear? The Lord says that He will raise him up."

At 8 o'clock they said to me, "Have a little refreshment." But I have found prayer and fasting the greatest joy, and you will always find it so when you are led by God. When we went to the house where Lazarus lived there were eight of us altogether. No one can prove to me that God does not always answer prayer. He always gives the exceeding abundant above all we ask or think.

I shall never forget how the power of God fell on us as we went into that sick man's room. Oh, it was lovely! As we circled round the bed I got one brother to hold the sick man's hand on one side and I held the other, and we each held the hand of the other next to us. I said, "We are not going to pray, we are just going to use the name of Jesus." We all knelt down and whispered that one word, "Jesus! Jesus! Jesus!" The power of God fell and then it lifted. Five times the power of God fell and then it remained. But the person who was in the bed was unmoved. Two years previous someone had come along and had tried to raise him up, and the devil had used his lack of success as a means of discouraging Lazarus. I said, "I don't care what the devil says; if God says he will raise you up it must be so. Forget everything else except what God says about Jesus."

The sixth time the power fell and the sick man's lips began moving and the tears began to fall. I said to him, "The power of God is here, it is yours to accept it." He said, "I have been bitter in my heart, and I know I have grieved the Spirit of God. Here I am helpless. I cannot lift my hands, nor even lift a spoon to my mouth." I said, "Repent, and God will hear you." He repented and cried out, "Oh God, let this be to Thy glory." As he said this the virtue of the Lord went right through him.

I have asked the Lord to never let me tell this story except as it was, for I realize that God can never bless exaggerations. As we again said, "Jesus! Jesus! Jesus!" the bed shook, and the man shook. I said to the people who were with me, "You can all go downstairs right away. This is all God. I'm not going to assist him." I sat and watched that man get up and dress himself. We sang the doxology as he walked down the steps. I said to him, "Now tell what has happened."

It was soon noised abroad that Lazarus had been raised up and the people came from Llanelli and all the district round to see him and hear his testimony. And God brought salvation to many. This man told right out in the open air what God had done, and as a result many were convicted and converted. All this came through the name of Jesus, through faith in His name, yea, the faith that is by Him gave this sick man perfect soundness in the presence of them all.

Peter and John were helpless, were illiterate, they had no college education. They had had some training with fish, and they had been with Jesus. To them had come a wonderful revelation of the power of the name of Jesus. They had handed out the bread and fish after Jesus had multiplied them. They had sat at the table with Him, and John had often gazed into His face. Peter had often to be rebuked, but Jesus manifested His love to Peter through it all. Yea, He loved Peter, the wayward one. Oh, He's a wonderful lover! I have been wayward, I have been stubborn, I had an unmanageable temper at one time, but how patient He has been. I am here to tell you that there is power in Jesus and in His wondrous name to transform anyone, to heal anyone.

If only you will see Him as God's Lamb, as God's beloved Son who had laid upon Him the iniquity of us all, if only you will see that Jesus paid the whole price for our redemption that we might be free, you can enter into your purchased inheritance of salvation, of life, and of power.

Poor Peter, and poor John! They had no money! I don't think there is a person in this building as poor as Peter and John. But they had faith, they had the power of the Holy Ghost, they had God. You can have God even though you have nothing else. Even though you have lost your character you can have God. I have seen the worst men saved by the power of God.

I was one day preaching about the name of Jesus and there was a man leaning against a lamppost, listening. It took a lamppost to enable him to keep on his feet. We had finished our open air meeting, and the man was still leaning against the post. I asked him, "Are you sick?" He showed me his hand, and I saw that beneath his coat, he had a silver handled dagger. He told me that he was on his way to kill his unfaithful wife, but that he had heard me speaking about the power of the name of Jesus and could not get away. He said that he felt just helpless. I said, "Get you down." And there on the square, with people passing up and down, he got saved.

I took him to my home and put on him a new suit. I saw that there was something in that man that God could use. He said to me the next morning, "God has revealed Jesus to me; I see that all has been laid upon Jesus." I lent him some money, and he soon got together a wonderful little home. His faithless wife was living with another man, but he invited her back to the home that he had prepared for her. She came: and, where enmity and hatred had been before, the whole situation was transformed by love. God made that man a minister wherever he went. There is power in the name of Jesus everywhere. God can save to the uttermost.

There comes before me a meeting we had in Stockholm that I shall ever bear in my mind. There was a home for incurables there and one of the inmates was brought to the meeting. He had palsy and was shaking all over. He stood up before 3,000 people and came to the platform, supported by two others. The power of God fell on him as I anointed him in the name of Jesus. The moment I touched him he dropped his crutch and began to walk in the name of Jesus. He walked down the steps and round that great building in view of all the people. There is nothing that our God cannot do. He will do everything if you will dare to believe.

Someone said to me, "Will you go to this Home for Incurables?" They took me there on my rest day. They brought out the sick people into a great corridor and in one hour the Lord set about 20 of them free.

The name of Jesus is so marvelous. Peter and John had no conception of all that was in that name; neither had the man, lame from his mother's womb who was laid daily at the gate; but they had faith to say, "In the name of Jesus Christ of Nazareth, rise up and walk." And as Peter took him by the right hand, and lifted him up, immediately his feet and ankle bones received strength, and he went into the temple with them, walking and leaping and praising God. God wants you to see more of this sort of thing done. How can it be done? Through His name, through faith in His name, through faith which is by Him.

Published in *The Pentecostal Evangel*

HOW TO ACT
ON GOD'S WORD
August 9, 1925

Acts 1:1-8. God means us to be in this way where Jesus went and all His disciples, He has left this place open. "Greater works than these shall ye do; because I go to my Father." Jesus left nothing less than this, a power which was for them and to which more was to be added if we believe.

We have recently had seven years of earthly power, and are feeling the effects of it today, how it has broken hearts, homes and in fact the whole world, and filled it with such distressing effects and made it an awful place, that we never want it again.

This power is so much different; it restores the fallen, it heals the brokenhearted, it lifts, it lives, it brings life into existence in your own hearts. All the time there is something that is round about you, something that you know is lasting and will be forever, until the Lord will receive us unto Himself.

God, help me to speak tonight, I came not to speak only but to stir us up to our privilege to make men feel they are responsible for the state of things round about.

POWER AND PROGRESS

It thrills my soul and makes me think that I must step into line where God has called me. Sometimes I speak like this, some of you know what a tragedy is, you have heard of such things, and some of you know what a calamity is. I speak to every baptized soul here tonight, if you have not made any progress, you are a backslider in the sight of God; because of the privilege of the revelation of the Spirit within you, privilege and more power of entering into more light.

It is a wonderful thing to get into touch with the living God, it is a glorious thing, a blessed condescension of God to fill us with the Holy Ghost. But the responsibility after that, for the Spirit of God, for Jesus to be so pleased with His child that He fills His child with the Holy Ghost; that the child may now have the full revelation of Himself, for the Holy Ghost shall not speak of Himself, but He shall take of the truth and reveal it unto us. As He is we have to be, and just as righteous as He is we have to be, we are truly the offspring of God, actuating with divine impulse, and God is proving us to see that we must step into line, and see that the truth is still the same.

"...Ye shall receive power..." (Acts 1:8). Brothers, it is so real, His life for me the life of the Son of God within, characteristics to make the whole body a flame of fire, after that ye shall receive power. I am clearly coming to understand this in my ministry, God has given me a gracious ministry and I thank God for it. God has given me a ministry which I prize because it helps me to stir people, especially leaders. I am here tonight to stir you, I could not think that God would have me leave you as I found you. If I thought I was entrusted to speak for half an hour, and leave you as I found you. So my desire is that this half hour shall be so full of divine purpose, that everyone shall come into line with the plan of God tonight.

POWER AND PURITY

I am as satisfied as anything that if I wait further, I have mistaken the position. On this line I so want to say things to prove the situation. There is a great deal too much on the lines of, "If I can only feel the power." Our young brother said distinctly that the Holy Ghost came to abide. What are we waiting for? What is God waiting for? For you to get into the place. What do I mean? I mean this: that Jesus was a perfect activity, a life in activity. The Scripture declares it. He began to do, and then to teach. It is as clear as possible, in a realm of divine appointment, where He was able to make the act conform.

So I am truly on the Word of God tonight, if we have received the power the power is there. I am not going to say, that there has not to be an unbroken fellowship with Him, He never separates power from holiness, the pure in heart shall see God. But I believe that if He has come to reveal unto us Him, you cannot lack it, because he who believes that Jesus is the Christ, overcomes the world.

He is the purifier, He is the abiding presence, the one great source of righteousness, then all the fullness of the Godhead bodily dwells in Him, there is the situation.

(Chorus: Christ liveth in me.)

And you know that after the Spirit gave the revelation of the purity of Christ by the Word of the Lord, He made you see things as you never saw them before.

I would like to speak for a few moments on the breath of the Spirit, because I see the Holy Spirit came as a breath, or as the moving of a mighty wind. I see so much divine appointment in this for humanity, this great thought, the Holy Spirit fills the life by the breath. It is wonderful—this prophetic position. Who did you hear speak? Yes, I hear Mr. Wigglesworth and Mr. Carter. Yes, that is the term. Behind it all you will find that language is breath.

When you are filled with the breath of the Spirit, the breath of God, the holy fire and the Word, it is Christ within you.

Life is given, he that heareth my words and believeth on Him that sent me hath everlasting life. We need the Spirit, to be filled with prophetic power to bring forth to the needs of the people, life. This is life that I am perceiving and I must be so in this order. Let me give you one or two positions.

POWER IN ACTION

God wants everybody, without exception, to begin on the Word of God, and to act. It will be the most surprising thing that ever came. As you stand on the Word it will be an amazing thing.

One day as I was going down the streets of San Francisco in a car, when looking through the window I saw a great crowd of people at the corner of the street. "Stop," I said, "there is something amiss," so I rushed as fast as possible to the edge of the crowd. I was so eager I pressed myself into the crowd, and I saw a boy laid on the ground who was held in a death-like grip.

The Word is in thee. I put my ear to his mouth as the boy lay there struggling. "Tell me, boy, what it is"; and the boy said, "It is cramp," so I put my hands around him, and said, "Come out in the Name of Jesus." The boy immediately jumped up, ran off and had no time to say thank you. It is for everyone. After that you have received you are in the place. I am not saying that glibly, my thoughts are too serious for that. **I cannot be any more after tonight what I was today, and tomorrow is mightier than today.** This is the reason the tide is changing with God. This is the reality.

It is no little thing to be baptized, it is the promise of the Father, Jesus must be there, and the Holy Ghost also bringing us to the place where we can be baptized. Are you going to treat it as a great thing? What do you really believe it is? I believe when the Holy Ghost comes that He comes to crown the King.

And the King from that day gets His rightful place, and we don't have to claim anything, and He becomes King of all the situations.

I only say this to help you. It is a need that I am speaking about, that I cannot get away from the fact, because where I look I see growth. I see you people, I see the growth, I have been away from England three years, and I see changes, and even though we see there is growth, life and blessing, there is much more ground to be possessed, and we shall have to dare before God can work.

God has given me an open door. Nothing moves me, only this, except I see men and women coming into line with this.

I want the people of Pentecost to rise as the heart of one man, God has us for a purpose in these last days, and in the meeting God helps me.

At a certain meeting, I said, "There is a man in this meeting suffering, and shall I preach before I help this man, or would you like to see this person free before I commence?" This man was a stranger and did not know who I was speaking about. There he was, with cancer on the face and full of pain, and I said, "Is it right to preach, or shall I heal this man?"

I saw what was the right thing, and I went down off the platform and placed my hand on him in the Name of Jesus.

This was because of what the Word said, that man knew nothing of healing, but in a moment he was able to stand up, and said, "I have been twelve years in pain, something has happened to me," and that night he gave himself to God, and testified night after night, that he was completely cured. What was it? God ministered through daring to believe His Word. There are cases round about you, and what a story you would have to tell next year if only people took a stand on the Word of God from tonight.

A woman brought her husband to me and said, "I want you to help my husband." I said, "Well, I will." She said, "He has too many complaints to tell you of."

[I said,] "There is a man here so full of pains and weakness that I am going to pray for him on the authority of God's Word, and tomorrow night I am going to ask him to come back and tell you what God has done for him." And I placed my hand on him in the Name of Jesus. The next night this man came walking straight, and he said, "Will you let me speak to these people tonight? For 40 years I have had ulcers and running sores, and today is the first day that my clothes have been dry, and now I am a new man." Brothers and sisters, this is declared in the Word, and wonderful things happen.

I had been speaking about divine healing, and six seats from the rear was a man with a boy and he lifted him up when I had finished. The boy was held together with irons, and his head, loins and shoulders were bandaged. The father handed him over to me.

There he put the irons down with the boy standing in them. I have never known what there is in the laying on of hands, let me give you a description of it. This boy was about nine years of age, and laying hands on him in the Name of Jesus, there was a perfect silence, when suddenly this boy cried out. "Dad, it is going all over me," and I said, "Take the irons off." You say that is our power. No, it is His power; no, it is the Father you have received. Dare we be still and be quiet, the stones would cry out if we did.

Sometimes I go in for what they call wholesale healings. My son and daughter are here, and they can declare that they have seen 100 healed without the touch a hand. I believe there is to be wholesale baptisms of the Holy Ghost. One day God told me something, at a place called Staranga in Norway.

I said to my interpreter, "We are both very tired. We will rest today until 4:00 p.m." I can never forget the sight; this story has just occurred to me. May God bend your ears down. There is a hearing of faith, a much higher faith. May the Lord bend our ears.

We had been out for a short time, and coming back into the street I shall never forget the sight. The street was filled with all kinds of wheelchairs, we went along up to the house, and the house was filled with people, and the woman said, "What can we do?"

"The house is filled, what are we to do?" So I pulled off my coat and I got to business. My brothers, you ought to have been there, the power of God came like a cloud and people were healed on every side.

God healed all the people. This is what I have to tell you. We were sat down for a little refresher before the meeting, and the telephone bell rang. And the pastor went to the telephone, and they said, "What can we do? The great Town Hall is packed. Come down as soon as you can." And this is what I mean by the hearing of faith: I declare that the people could not have fallen down if they had wanted to. I never saw a place so packed, and I began to preach, and when I was preaching the voice came from the Lord.

"Ask and I will give thee every soul." The voice came again, "Ask and I will give you every soul," and I dared to ask, "Give me every soul," and there was a breath came like the rushing of a mighty wind, and it shook everybody and fell on everyone. I have never seen anything like it.

I am hoping to see this in London. Is there anything too hard for God? Cannot God begin to do these things? Will we let Him?

I know it might be a difficult thing. Is it not possible to have a consecration tonight? Who is there who will begin tonight and begin to act in the power of the Holy Ghost?

Address given at Second Annual Convention of the Assemblies of God
Kingsway Hall

THE PENTECOSTAL POWER
November 12, 1927

Acts 19:1-20. This is a wonderful reading. It has many things in it which indicate to us that there was something more marvelous about it than human power, and when I think about Pentecost I am astonished from day to day because of its mightiness, of its wonderfulness and how the glory overshadows it. I think sometimes about these things and they make me feel we have only just touched it. Truly it is so, but we must thank God that we have touched it. We must not give in because we have only touched. Whatever God has done in the past, His name is still the same. When hearts are burdened and they come face to face with the need of the day, they look into God's Word and it brings in a propeller of power or an anointing that makes you know He has truly visited. It was a wonderful day when Jesus left the glory. I can imagine all the angels and God the Father and all heaven so wonderfully stirred that day when the angels were sent to tell that wonderful story: "Peace on earth and good will to men." It was a glorious day when they beheld the Babe for the first time and God was looking on. What happened after that day and until He was 30 years old I suppose it would take a big book to put it all in. It was a working up to a great climax.

I know that Pentecost in my life is a working up to a climax. It is not all done in a day. There are many waters and all kinds of times until we get to the real summit of everything. The power of God is here to prevail. God is with us. The mother of Jesus hid a lot of things in her heart. The time came when it was made manifest at Jordan that Jesus was the Son of God. Oh, how beautifully it was made known! It had to be made known first to one that was full of the vision of God. The vision comes to those who are full. Did it ever strike you we cannot be too full for a vision, we cannot have too much of God? The more of God, then the visions begin. When God has you in His own plan, what a change, how things operate. You wonder, you see things in a new light. And how God is being glorified as you yield from day to day, and the Spirit seems to lay hold of you and bring you on. Yes, it is pressing on, and then He gives us touches of His wonderful power, manifestations of the glory of these things and indications of great things to follow, and these days which we are living in now speak of better days. How wonderful!

Where should we have been today if we had stopped short, if we had not fulfilled the vision which God gave us? I am thinking about that time when Christ sent the Spirit; and Paul did not know much about that, his heart was stirred, his eyes were dim, he was going to put the whole thing to an end in a short time, and Jesus was looking on. We can scarcely understand the whole process only as God seems to show us, when He gets us into His plan and works with us little by little. We are all amazed that we are amongst the "tongues people," it is altogether out of order according to the natural. Some of us would have never been in this Pentecostal movement had we not been drawn, but God has a wonderful way of drawing us. Paul never intended to be among the disciples, Paul never intended to have anything to do with this Man called Jesus, but God was working. God has been working with us and has brought us to this place. It is marvelous! Oh! the vision of God, the wonderful manifestation which God has for Israel.

I have one purpose in my heart, and it is surely God's plan for me, that I want you to see that Jesus Christ is the greatest manifestation in all the world, and His power is unequaled, but there is only one way to minister it. I want you to notice that these people, after they had seen Paul working wonders by this power, began on a natural line. I see it is necessary for me if I want to do anything for God, I must get the knowledge of God, I must get the vision of God, I cannot work on my own. It must be a divine revelation of the Son of God. It must be that. I can see as clearly as anything that Paul in his mad pursuit had to be stopped in the way, and after he was stopped in the way and had the vision from heaven and that light from heaven, instantly he realized that he had been working the wrong way. And as soon as ever the power of the Holy Ghost fell upon him, he began in the way in which God wanted him to go. And it was wonderful how he had to suffer to come into the way. It is broken spirits, it is tried lives, and it is being driven into a corner as if some strange thing had happened, that is, surely the way to get to know the way of God.

Paul had not any power to use the name of Jesus as he did use it, only as he had to go through the privations and the difficulties, and even when all things seemed as though shipwrecked, God stood by him and made him know that there was something behind all the time that was with him, and able to carry him through, and bring out that for which his heart was all the time longing. Unconsciously he seemed to be so filled with the Holy Ghost that all that was needed was just the bringing of the aprons and the handkerchiefs and sending them forth. I can imagine these people looking on and seeing him and saying, "But it is all in the name, don't you notice that when he sends the handkerchiefs and the aprons he says, 'In the name of the Lord Jesus I command that evil to come out'?"

These people had been looking round and watching, and they thought, "It is only the name, that is all that is needed," and so these men said, "We will do the same." These vagabond Jews, those seven sons of Sceva, were determined to make this thing answer, and they came to the place where that man had been for years possessed with an evil power, and as they entered in they said, "We adjure thee in the name of Jesus to come out." The demons said, "Jesus we know, and Paul we know, but who are ye?" and this evil power leaped upon them and tore their things off their backs, and they went out naked and wounded. (See Acts 19:13-17.) It was the name, only they did not understand it. Oh, that God should help us to understand the name! It is the name, oh, it is still the name. But you must understand there is the ministry of the name, there is something in the name that makes the whole world charmed. It is the Holy Spirit back of the ministry, it is the knowledge of Him, it is the ministry of the knowledge of Him, and I can understand it is only that.

I want to speak about the ministry of the knowledge; it is important. God, help us to see. I am satisfied with two things; one is this, I am satisfied it is the knowledge of the blood of Jesus Christ today, and the knowledge of His perfect holiness. I am perfectly cleansed from all sin and made holy in the knowledge of His holiness. I am satisfied today that as I know Him, and the knowledge of His power, and the Christ that is manifested, and the power that worketh in me to minister as I am ministering only in the knowledge of it, it is effective, so that it brings out the very thing which the Word of God says it will do, in the ministry of which, as I know it, it has power over all evil powers by its effectual working in that way. I minister today in the power of the knowledge of the ministry of it, and beyond that there is a certain sense that I overcome the world according to my faith in Him, and I am more than a conqueror over everything just in the knowledge that I have of Him being over everything, as crowned by the Father to bring everything into subjection. Shouting won't do it, but there is a lubrication about it which is gloriously felt within and brings it into perfect harmony with the will of God, but it is not in the shout, and yet we cannot help but shout, but it is in the ministry of the knowledge that He is Lord over all demons, all powers of wickedness.

TONGUES AND INTERPRETATION: "The Holy One which anointed Jesus is so abiding by the Spirit in the one that is clothed upon to use the name till the glory is manifested and the demons flee, they cannot stand the glory of the manifestation of the Spirit which is manifest."

So I am realizing that Paul went about clothed in the Spirit. This was wonderful, His body was full of virtue? No!! He sent forth handkerchiefs from his body and aprons from his body, and when they touched the needy, they were healed and demons were cast out. Virtue in his body? No! Virtue in Jesus by the ministry of faith in the name of Jesus through the power of the unction of the Holy Ghost in Paul.

TONGUES AND INTERPRETATION: "The liberty of the Spirit bringeth the office."

It is an office, it is a position, it is a place of rest, of faith. Sometimes the demon powers are dealt with very differently, not all the same way: but the ministry of the Spirit by which it is ministered by the power of the word "Jesus" never fails to accomplish the purpose for which the one in charge has wisdom or discernment to see, because along with the Spirit of ministry there comes the revelation of the need of the needy one that is bound.

So differently the Spirit ministers the name of Jesus. I see it continually happening. I see those things answer and all the time the Lord is building up a structure of His own power by a living faith in the knowledge of the sovereignty of the name of Jesus. If I turn to John's gospel I get the whole thing practically in a nutshell. To know Thee, O God, and Jesus Christ whom Thou hast sent, is eternal life. We must have the knowledge and power of God and the knowledge of Jesus Christ, the embodiment of God, to be clothed upon with God, God in human flesh. I see there are those who have come into line, they are possessed with the blessed Christ, and the power of the baptism which is the revelation of the Christ of God within, and it is so evidently in the person who is baptized and the Christ is so plainly abiding that the moment he is confronted with evil, instantly he is sensitive of the position of this confronting, and he is able to deal accordingly.

The difference between the sons of Sceva and Paul is this: They said, "It is only using the word." How many people only use the word, how many times people are defeated because they think it is just the word, how many people have been brokenhearted because it did not answer when they used the word? If I read into my text this afternoon this, "He that believeth shall speak in tongues, he that believeth shall cast out devils, he that believeth shall lay hands on the sick," if I read this into my text, on the surface of it, it seems exactly easy, but you must understand this, there are volumes to be applied to the word *believe.* To believe is to believe in the need of the majesty of the glory of the power, which is all power, which brings all other powers into subjection.

And what is belief? Sum it up in a few sentences. To believe is to have the knowledge of Him in whom you believe, it is not to believe in the word Jesus, but to believe in the nature, to believe in the vision, for all power is given unto Him, and greater is He that is within thee in the revelation of faith than he that is in the world, and so I say to you, do not be discouraged if every demon has not gone out. The very moment you have gone, do not think there is an end of it. What we have to do is to see this, that if it had only been using the name, those evil powers would have gone out in that name by the sons of Sceva. It is not that. It is the virtue of the power of the Holy Ghost, with the revelation of the deity of our Christ of glory, where all power is given unto Him, and in the knowledge of Christ, in the faith of what He is, demons must surrender, demons must go out, and I say it reverently, these bodies of ours are so constructed by God that we may be filled with that divine revelation of the Son of God till it is manifest to the devils you go to and they have to go. The Master is in. They see the Master. Jesus I know, and Paul I know. The ministry of the Master! How we need to get to know Him till within us we are full of the manifestation of the King over all demons.

Brothers and sisters, my heart is full. The depths of my yearnings are for the Pentecostal people. My cry is that we will not miss the opportunity of the baptism of the Holy Ghost, that Christ may be manifested in the human till every power of evil will be subject to the Christ which is manifested in you. The devils know. Two important things are before me. To master the situation of myself. You are not going to meet devils if you cannot master yourself, because you soon find the devil bigger than yourself, and it is only when you are subdued that Christ is enthroned and the embodiment of the Spirit is so gloriously covering the human life that Jesus is glorified to the full. So first it is the losing of ourself and then it is the incoming of Another; it is the glorifying of Him which is to fulfill all things and when He gets lives He can do it. When He gets lives that will so yield themselves to God, God will be delighted to allow the Christ to be so manifested in you, that it will be no difficulty for the devil to know who you are.

I am satisfied that Pentecost is to reestablish God in human flesh. Do I need to say it again? The power of the Holy Ghost has to come to be enthroned in the human life so it does not matter what state we are in. Christ is manifested in the place where devils are, the place where religious devils are, the place where a false religion and unbelief are, the place where a formal religion has taken the place of holiness and righteousness. You have need to have holiness, the righteousness and Spirit of the Master, so that in every walk of life everything that is not like our Lord Jesus will have to depart and that is what is needed today. I ask you in the Holy Ghost to seek the place where He is in power. "Jesus I know, Paul I know but who are ye?" May God stamp it upon us for the devil is not afraid of you. May the Holy Ghost make us today terrors of evildoers, for the Holy Ghost came into us to judge the world of sin, of unbelief, of righteousness, and that is the purpose of the Holy Ghost. The devils will know us, and Jesus will know us.

Published in *The Pentecostal Evangel*

HEAVENLY POWER
May 27, 1944

We have a remarkable word in Matthew 3:11,

I indeed baptize you with water unto repentance: but he that cometh after me is mightier than I, whose shoes I am not worthy to bear: he shall baptize you with the Holy Ghost, and with fire.

This was the word of one who was filled with the Holy Ghost even from his mother's womb, who was so filled with the power of the Spirit of God that they came from east and west and from north and south to the banks of the Jordan to hear him.

You have seen water baptism, and you know what it means. This later baptism taught by this wilderness preacher means that we shall be so immersed, covered, and flooded with the blessed Holy Ghost, that He fills our whole body.

Now turn to John 7:37-39:

In the last day, that great day of the feast, Jesus stood and cried, saying, If any man thirst, let him come unto me, and drink. He that believeth on me, as the scripture hath said, out of his belly shall flow rivers of living water. (But this spake he of the Spirit, which they

223

that believe on him should receive: for the Holy Ghost was not yet given; because that Jesus was not yet glorified.)

John 7:37-39

Jesus saw that the people who had come to the feast, expecting blessing, were going back dissatisfied. He had come to help the needy, to bring satisfaction to the unsatisfied. He does not want any of us to be thirsty, famished, naked, full of discord, full of disorder, full of evil, full of carnality, full of sensuality. And so He sends out in His own blessed way the old prophetic cry: "Ho, every one that thirsteth, come ye to the waters, and he that hath no money; come ye, buy, and eat..." (Isa. 55:1).

The Master can give you that which will satisfy. He has in Himself just what you need at this hour. He knows your greatest need. You need the blessed Holy Ghost, not merely to satisfy your thirst, but to satisfy the needs of thirsty ones everywhere; for as the blessed Holy Spirit flows through you like rivers of living water, these floods will break what needs to be broken, they will bring to death that which should be brought to death, but they will bring life and fruitage where there is none.

What do you have? A well of water? That is good as far as it goes. But Christ wants to see a plentiful supply of the river of the Holy Ghost flowing through you. Here, on this last day of the feast, we find Him preparing them for the Pentecostal fullness that was to come, the fullness that He should shed forth from the glory after His ascension.

Note the condition necessary—"He that believeth on Me." This is the root of the matter. Believe on Him. Believing on Him will bring forth this river of blessedness. Abraham believed God, and we are all blessed through faithful Abraham. As we believe God, many will be blessed through our faith. Abraham was an extraordinary man of faith. He believed God in the face of everything. God wants to bring us to the place of believing, where, despite all contradictions around, we are strong in faith, giving God glory. As we fully believe God, He will be glorified, and we will prove a blessing to the whole world as was our father Abraham.

Turn to John 14. Here we see the promise that ignorant and unlearned fishermen were to be clothed with the Spirit, anointed with power from on High, and endued with the Spirit of wisdom and knowledge. As He imparts divine wisdom, you will not act foolishly. The Spirit of God will give you a sound mind, and He will impart to you the divine nature.

How could these weak and helpless fishermen, poor and needy, ignorant and unlearned, do the works of Christ and greater works than He had done? They were incapable. None of us is able. But our emptiness has to be clothed with divine fullness, and our helplessness has to be filled with the power of His helpfulness. Paul knew this when he gloried in all that brought him down in weakness, for flowing into his weakness came a mighty deluge of divine power.

Christ knew that His going away would leave His disciples like a family of orphans. But He told them it was expedient, it was best, for after His return to the Father He would send the Comforter, and He Himself would come to indwell them. "...ye in me, and I in you" (John 14:20).

Christ said, "And I will pray the Father, and he shall send you another Comforter, that he may abide with you for ever; even the Spirit of truth..." (John 14:16,17). What a fitting name for the One who was coming to them at the time they were bereft—Comforter. After Christ had left them there was a great need, but that need was met on the day of Pentecost when the Comforter came.

You will always find that in the moment of need the Holy Spirit is a comforter. When my dear wife was lying dead, the doctors could do nothing. They said to me, "She's gone; we cannot help you." My heart was so moved that I said, "Oh God, I cannot spare her!" I went up to her and said, "Oh, come back, come back, and speak to me! Come back, come back!" The Spirit of the Lord moved, and she came back and smiled again. But then the Holy Ghost said to me, "She's mine. Her work is done. She is mine."

Oh, that comforting word! No one else could have spoken it. The Comforter came. From that moment my dear wife passed out. And in this day the Comforter has a word for every bereaved one.

Christ further said,

> *But the Comforter, which is the Holy Ghost, whom the Father will send in my name, he shall teach you all things, and bring all things to your remembrance, whatsoever I have said unto you.*
>
> *John 14:26*

How true this is. From time to time He takes of the words of Christ and makes them life to us. And, empowered with this blessed Comforter, the words that we spake under the anointing are spirit and life.

There are some who come to our meetings who, when you ask them whether they are seekers, reply, "Oh, I am ready for anything." I tell them, "You will never get anything." It is necessary to have the purpose that the psalmist had when he said, "One thing have I desired of the Lord, that will I seek after..." (Ps. 27:4). When the Lord reveals to you that you must be filled with the Holy Ghost, seek that one thing until God gives you that gift.

I spoke to two young men in a meeting one day. They were preachers. They had received their degrees. I said to them, "Young men, what about it?"

"Oh," they said, "we do not believe in receiving the Holy Ghost in the same way as you people do."

I said to them, "You are dressed up like preachers, and it is a pity having to have the dress without the presence."

"Well, we do not believe it the way you do," they said.

"But look," I said, "the apostles believed it that way. Wouldn't you like to be like the apostles? You have read how they received at the beginning, haven't you?"

Always remember this, that the baptism will always be as at the beginning. It has not changed. If you want a real baptism, expect it just the same way as they had it at the beginning.

These preachers asked, "What had they at the beginning?"

I quoted from the tenth chapter of Acts where it says,

...on the Gentiles also was poured out the gift of the Holy Ghost.
For they heard them speak with tongues, and magnify God....

Acts 10:45, 46

The Jews knew that these Gentiles had the same kind of experience as they themselves had at the beginning on the day of Pentecost. The experience has not changed, it is still the same as at the beginning.

When these two young men realized that Peter and John and the rest of the disciples had received the mighty enduement at the beginning, and that it was for them, they walked up to the front where folk were tarrying. They were finely dressed, but in about half an hour they looked different. They had been prostrated. I had not caused them to do it. But they had been so lost and so controlled by the power of God, and were so filled with the glory of God, they just rolled over, and their fine clothes were soiled—but their faces were radiant. What caused the change? They had received what the 124 received at the beginning.

These young preachers had been ordained by men. Now they received an ordination that was better. The Lord had ordained them that they should go and bring forth much fruit. The person who receives this ordination goes forth with fresh feet—his feet shod with the preparation of the Gospel of peace; he goes forth with a fresh voice—it speaks as the Spirit gives utterance; he goes forth with a fresh mind—a mind illuminated by the power of God; he goes forth with a fresh vision, and sees all things new.

When I was in Switzerland, a woman came to me and said, "Now that I am healed and have been delivered from that terrible carnal oppression that bound and fettered me, I feel that I have a new mind. I should like to receive the Holy Ghost; but when I hear these people at the altar making so much noise, I feel like running away."

Shortly after this we were in another place in Switzerland where there was a great hotel joined to the building where we were ministering. At the close of one of the morning services, the power of God fell. That is the only way I can describe it—the power of God fell. This poor, timid creature, who could not bear to hear any noise, screamed so loud that all the waiters in this big hotel came out, with their aprons on and their trays, to see what was up. Nothing especially was "up," something had come down, and it so altered the situation that this woman could stand anything after that.

When you receive the baptism, remember the words in 1 John 2:20. "...ye have an unction from the Holy One...." God grant that we may not forget that. Many people, instead of standing on the rock of faith to believe that they have received this unction, say, "Oh, if I could only feel the unction!"

Brother, your feeling robs you of your greatest unction. Your feelings are often on the line of discouragement. You have to get away from the walk by sense, for God has said, "The just shall live by faith" (Hab. 2:4; Rom. 1:17; Gal. 3:11; and Heb. 10:38). Believe what God says, "Ye have an unction from the Holy One," an unction from above. All thoughts of holiness, all thoughts of purity, all thoughts of power are from above.

Frequently I see a condition of emergency. Here is a woman dying; here is a man who has lost all the powers of his faculties; here is a person apparently in death. God does not want me to be filled with anxiety. What does He want me to do? To *believe* only. After you have received, Only believe. Dare to believe the One who has declared, "I will do it." Christ says,

> ...*verily I say unto you, That whosoever shall say unto this mountain, Be thou removed, and be thou cast into the sea; and shall not doubt in his heart, but shall believe that those things which he saith shall come to pass; he shall have whatsoever he saith.*
>
> *Mark 11:23*

God declares, "Ye have an unction." Believe God, and you will see this happen. What you say will come to pass. Speak the Word and the bound shall be free, the sick shall be healed. "...he shall have whatsoever he saith" (Mark 11:23). "Ye have an unction." The unction has come, the unction abides, the unction is with us.

But what about it, if you have not lived in the place where the unction can be increased? What is the matter? There is something between you and the Holy One—some uncleanness, some impurity, some desire that is not of Him, something that has come in the way? The Spirit is grieved. Has the unction left? No. When He comes in, He comes to abide. Make confession of your sin, of your failure, and once more the precious blood of Jesus Christ will cleanse, and the grieved Spirit will once more manifest Himself.

John further says, "...the anointing which ye have received of him abideth in you..." (1 John 2:27). We have an anointing, the same anointing which Jesus Christ Himself received. For "God anointed Jesus of Nazareth with the Holy Ghost and with power: who went about doing good..." (Acts 10:38). The same anointing is for us.

It means much to have a continuous faith for the manifestation of the anointing. At the death of Lazarus, when it seemed that Mary and Martha and all around them had lost faith, Jesus turned to the Father and said, "Father, I thank thee that thou hast heard me. And I knew that thou hearest me always..." (John 11:41,42). Before that supreme faith that counted on God that counted on His anointing, death had to give up Lazarus.

Through a constant fellowship with the Father, through bold faith in the Son, through a mighty unction of the blessed Holy Spirit, there will come a right of way for God to be enthroned in your hearts, purifying us so thoroughly that there is no room for anything but the divine presence within. And through the manifestation of this presence, the works of Christ and greater works shall be accomplished for the glory of our triune God.

Published in *The Pentecostal Evangel*

LIVING IN THE POWER

Abide in the presence of power where victory is assured. If we keep in the right place with God, God can do anything with us. There is a power and majesty falling on Jesus. He is no longer the same. He has now received the mighty anointing power of God. And He realizes submission, and as He submits He is more and more covered with the power and led by the Spirit. He came out of the wilderness more full of God, more clothed with the Spirit and ready for the fight. The enduement with power had such an effect upon Him that other people saw it and flocked to hear Him, and great blessing came to the land.

The Holy Ghost coming upon an individual changes him and fertilizes his spiritual life. What is possible if we reach this place and keep in it—abide in it. Only one thing is going to accomplish the purpose of God—that is, to be filled with the Spirit we must yield and submit, until our bodies are saturated with God, that at any moment God's will can be revealed. We want a great hunger and thirst for God.

Thousands must be brought to a knowledge of the truth; that will only be brought about by human instrumentality, when the instrument is at a place where he will say all the Holy Ghost directs him to; be still and know that I am God, the place of tranquility, where we know He is controlling, and moves us by the mighty power of His Spirit.

Ezekiel said, "I prophesied as I was commanded." He did what he was told to do. It takes more to live in that place than any other I know of. To live in the place where you hear God's voice. Only by the power of the Spirit can you do as you are told quickly.

We must keep at the place where we see God, always hearing His voice—where He sends us with messages bringing life and power and victory.

POWER FROM ON HIGH

"Ye shall receive power, after that the Holy Ghost is come upon you..." (Acts 1:8). The disciples had been asking whether the Lord would at that time restore again the kingdom to Israel. Christ told them that it was not for them to know the times and seasons which the Father had put in His own power, but He promised them that when they received the Holy Ghost they should receive power to witness for Him in all the world. To receive the Holy Ghost is to receive power with God, and power with men.

POWER FROM ON HIGH

There is a power of God and there is a power which is of satan. When the Holy Spirit fell in the early days, a number of spiritists came to our meetings. They thought we had received something like they had and they were coming to have a good time. They filled the two front rows of our mission. When the power of God fell, these imitators began their shaking and muttering under the power of the devil. The Spirit of the Lord came mightily upon me and I cried, "Now, you devils, clear out of this!" And out they went. I followed them right out into the street and then they turned round and cursed me. There was power from below, but it was no match for the power of the Holy Ghost, and they soon had to retreat.

The Lord wants all saved people to receive power from on High—power to witness, power to act, power to live, and power to show forth the divine manifestation of God within. The power of God will take you out of your own plans and put you into the plan of God. You will be unmantled and divested of that which is purely of yourself and put into a divine order. The Lord will change you and put His mind where yours was, and thus enable you to have the mind of Christ. Instead of your laboring according to your own plan, it will be God working in you and through you to do His own good pleasure through the power of the Spirit within. Someone has said that you are no good until you have your "I" knocked out. Christ must reign within, and the life in the Holy Ghost means at all times the subjection of your own will to make way for the working out of the good and acceptable and perfect will of God within.

The Lord Jesus gave commandment that the disciples should tarry until they were endued with power from on High and in Acts 2 we read how the Spirit of God came. He comes the same way today and we don't know of the Holy Ghost coming any other way.

I was holding a meeting, once, in London, and at the close a man came to me and said, "We are not allowed to hold meetings in this hall after 11 o'clock, and we would like you to come home with us, I am so hungry for God." The wife said she, too, was hungry, and so I agreed to go with them. At about 12:30 we arrived at their house. The man began stirring up the fire and said, "Now we will have a good supper." I said to them, "I did not come here for your warm fire, your supper, or your bed. I came here because I thought you were hungry to get more of God." We got down to pray and at about 3:30 the Lord baptized the wife, and she spoke in tongues as the Spirit gave utterance. At about 5 o'clock I spoke to the husband and asked how he was getting on. He replied, "God has broken my iron, stubborn will." He had not received the baptism, but God had wrought a mighty work within him.

The following day, at his business, everyone could tell that a great change had come to him. Before he had been a walking terror. The men who labored for him had looked upon him as a regular devil because of the way he had acted; but coming into contact with the power of God that night completely changed him. Before this he had made a religious profession, but he had never truly entered into the experience of the new birth until that night, when the power of God surged so mightily through his home. A short while afterward I went to this man's home, and his two sons ran to me and kissed me, saying, "We have a new father." Previous to this these boys had often said to their mother, "Mother, we cannot stand it in the home any longer. We will have to leave." But the Lord changed the whole situation that night as we prayed together. On the second visit the Lord baptized this man in the Holy Ghost. The Holy Spirit will reveal false positions, pull the mask off any refuge of lies and clean up and remove all false conditions. When the Holy Spirit came in, that man's house and business and he himself were entirely changed.

An Effective Witness

When the Holy Spirit comes He comes to empower you to be an effective witness. At one time we were holding some special meetings and I was out distributing bills. I went into a shoemaker's store and there was a man with a green shade over his eyes and also a cloth. My heart looked up to the Lord and I had the witness within that He was ready to change any condition. The man was crying, "Oh! Oh!! Oh!!!" I asked, "What's the trouble?" He told me he was suffering with great inflammation and burning. I said, "I rebuke this condition in Jesus' name." Instantly the Lord healed him. He took off the shade and cloth and said, "Look, it is all gone." I believe the Lord wants us to enter into real activity and dare to do for Him. "Ye shall receive power after that the Holy Ghost is come upon you."

At one time a lady wrote and asked if I could go and help her. She said that she was blind, having two blood clots behind her eyes. When I reached the house they brought the blind woman to me. We were together for some time and then the power of God fell. Rushing to the window she exclaimed, "I can see! Oh, I can see! The blood is gone, I can see." She then inquired about receiving the Holy Spirit and confessed that for ten years she had been fighting our position. She said, "I could not bear these tongues, but God has settled the whole thing today. I now want the baptism in the Holy Ghost." The Lord graciously baptized her in the Spirit.

The Holy Spirit will come when a man is cleansed. There must be a purging of the old life. I never saw anyone baptized who was not clean within. I never saw a man baptized who smoked. We take it for granted that anyone who is seeking the fullness of the Spirit is free from such things as these. You cannot expect the Third Person of the Trinity to come into an unclean temple. There first must be a confession of all that is wrong and a cleansing in the precious blood of Jesus Christ.

I remember being in a meeting at one time, where there was a man seeking the baptism, and he looked like he was in trouble. He was very restless, and finally he said to me, "I will have to go." I said, "What's up?" He said, "God is unveiling things to me, and I feel so unworthy." I said, "Repent of everything that is wrong." He continued to tarry and the Lord continued to search his heart. These times of waiting on God for the fullness of the Spirit are times when He searches the heart and tries the reins. Later the man said to me, "I have a hard thing to do, the hardest thing I have ever had to do." I said to him, "Tell the Lord you will do it, and never mind the consequences." He agreed, and the next morning he had to take a ride of 30 miles and go with a bag of gold to a certain party with whom he dealt. This man had 100 head of cattle and he bought all his feed at a certain place. He always paid his accounts on a certain day, but one day he missed. He was always so punctual in paying his accounts that when later the people of his firm went over their books, they thought they must have made a mistake in not crediting the man with the money and so they sent him a receipt. The man never intended not to pay the account, but if you defer to do a right thing the devil will see that you never do it. But when that man was seeking the Lord that night the Lord dealt with him on this point, and he had to go and straighten the thing the next morning. He paid the account and then the Lord baptized him in the Spirit. They that bear the vessels of the Lord must be clean, must be holy.

When the Holy Spirit comes He always brings a rich revelation of Christ. Christ becomes so real to you that, when, under the power of the Spirit, you begin to express your love and praise to Him, you find yourself speaking in another tongue. Oh, it is a wonderful thing! At one time I belonged to a class who believed that they had received the baptism in the Spirit without the speaking in tongues. There are many folks like that today, but if you can go with them to a prayer meeting you will find them asking the Lord again and again to baptize them in the Spirit. Why all this asking if they really have received the baptism? I have never heard anyone who has received the baptism in the Holy Ghost after the original pattern asking the Lord to give them the Holy Ghost. They know of a surety that He has come.

I was once traveling from Belgium to England. As I landed I received a request to stop at a place between Harwich and Colchester. The people were delighted that God had sent me, and told me of a special case they wanted me to pray for. They said, "We have a brother here who believes in the Lord, and he is paralyzed from his loins downward.

He cannot stand on his legs and he has been 20 years in this condition." They took me to this man and as I saw him there in his chair I put the question to him, is the greatest desire in your heart?" He said, "Oh, if I could only receive the Holy Ghost!" I was somewhat surprised at this answer, and I laid my hands on his head and said, "Receive ye the Holy Ghost." Instantly the power of God fell upon him and he began breathing very heavily. He rolled off the chair and there he lay like a bag of potatoes, utterly helpless. I like anything that God does. I like to watch God working. There he was with his great, fat body, and his head was working just as though it was on a swivel. Then to our joy he began speaking in tongues. I had my eyes on every bit of him and as I saw the condition of his legs I said, "Those legs can never carry that body." Then I looked up and said, "Lord, tell me what to do." The Holy Ghost is the executive of Jesus Christ and the Father. If you want to know the mind of God you must have the Holy Ghost to bring God's latest thought to you and to tell you what to do. The Lord said to me, "Command him in My name to walk." But I missed it, of course. I said to the people there, "Let's see if we can lift him up." But we could not lift him, he was like a ton weight. I cried, "Oh Lord, forgive me." I repented of doing the wrong thing, and then the Lord said to me again, "Command him to walk." I said to him, "Arise in the name of Jesus." His legs were immediately strengthened. Did he walk? He ran all round. A month after this he walked ten miles and back. He has a Pentecostal work now. When the power of the Holy Ghost is present, things will happen.

There is more for us all yet, praise the Lord. This is only the beginning. So far we have only touched the fringe of things. There is so much more for us if we will but yield to God.

Do you want to receive the Spirit?

If ye then, being evil, know how to give good gifts unto your children: how much more shall your heavenly Father give the Holy Spirit to them that ask him?

Luke 11:13

I am a father and I want to give my boys the very best. We human fathers are but finite, but our heavenly Father is infinite. There is no limit to the power and blessing He has laid up for them who love Him. Be filled with the Spirit.

AUTHOR CONTACT INFORMATION

Roberts Liardon Ministries

P.O. Box 30710

Laguna Hills, CA 92654

Phone: 949-833-3555

Fax: 949-833-9555

Web: www.robertsliardon.org

Official site of Smith Wigglesworth:

www.smithwigglesworth.org

Additional copies of this book and other
book titles from DESTINY IMAGE are
available at your local bookstore.

Call toll-free: 1-800-722-6774.

Send a request for a catalog to:

Destiny Image® Publishers, Inc.
P.O. Box 310
Shippensburg, PA 17257-0310

*"Speaking to the Purposes of God for This
Generation and for the Generations to Come"*

**For a complete list of our titles,
visit us at www.destinyimage.com**